THE GRIT

by

Jack Rose

and

Dean Parkin

THE GRIT

by

Jack Rose

and

Dean Parkin

*"It was a community on its own, but though they call it
the 'Beach' now, what we called it was 'The Grit' . . .
We used to say we were born on The Grit."*

LENNY 'WINKY' NORMAN

Rushmere
Publishing

First published 1997 by Rushmere Publishing
32 Rushmere Road, Carlton Colville, Lowestoft, Suffolk

Typeset by Chemtech Graphics
Sussex Road, Gorleston, Great Yarmouth, Norfolk

Printed in England by Blackwell John Buckle
Charles Street, Great Yarmouth, Norfolk NR30 3LA

ISBN 1 872992 10 2

This book is dedicated to
all those who lived on
The Grit

Contents

Acknowledgements

We would like to thank everybody who has helped with this publication, those who spoke or wrote to us, those who lent photographs and those who have put us in contact with others or pointed us in the right direction.

We are also grateful to Bert Collyer for his photographic work, Ernie Childs of Great Yarmouth Pottery for permission to reproduce his paintings on the cover, Molly O'Shane for the use of her postcard collection, Ivan Bunn for the maps, Anna Hogan for the drawings of 'Posh' Fletcher and Edward Fitzgerald, David Johnson for the modern photographs and Robin Summers for the loan of rare documents.

A special acknowledgement must be given to Christine Johnson for all her work on this book.

PICTURE CREDITS

Most of the photographs in this volume are from Jack Rose's own collection. The publishers are most grateful to the following who have kindly permitted the use of copyright material: Glennis Barnard; Matthew Boardley; Olive Burwood; Vina Capps-Jenner; Harry Collins; Lydia Cullen; Claude Dalley; Alan Doy; Ray Durrant; Iris Gibbs; Roger Gouldby; Oliver Guymer; Jessie Hitter; Ron James; David Johnson; Ada Jones; Billy Keith; Benny Knights; Peter Larter; Bob Malster; Ivan Meadows; Edna Mortensen; Charles Oldman; George Osborne; Joy Pearce; Bert Prettyman; Ian G. Robb; Clifford Temple and Alan Weller.

Introduction

Compiling this book has been like working on an enormous jigsaw. The idea for it arose from the first Beach Village exhibition which took place at Christ Church in 1995 where people began to ask about the possibility of a long overdue book devoted to the subject.

Once we decided to go ahead with the project, the framework was provided by notes gathered from many years of research, in addition to newspaper articles, essays and booklets from authors long since dead, such as Hugh Lees, whose research proved invaluable. The appeals for information, photographs and recollections, which were made at Beach reunions and in the Lowestoft Journal, proved fruitful and soon letters began to arrive and contacts were made. Dozens of interviews followed, hours of tape recordings and tens of thousands of words. Of course many of these stories overlapped and therefore needed editing, but piece by piece they fell into place and a true picture of the Beach began to emerge. With the book still growing and more people getting in touch, suggested publication dates came and went, and for a time it seemed as though we would never finish!

The people we spoke to are the last generation of 'Gritsters'. Jack grew up amongst these people who were children when they lived on the Beach and although aware that life was hard for their parents, they at least enjoyed the benefits and security of growing up in a close-knit community. We realise that had this book been attempted whilst their parents were alive, the story may have been rather different. Nonetheless, the importance of a record of this unique community was sadly illustrated by the death of several contributors during the preparation of the book.

Though there are still pieces of the jigsaw missing, possibly lost forever, we trust that this book gives a faithful account of what life was really like on the Beach. Our thanks to all the Gritsters who contacted us and were so willing to help. Their friendly nature is still very much in evidence and their stories and history at last captured in this book.

Jack Rose & Dean Parkin
September 1997

1

The Grit Swept Away

*"I was like most of the Beach boys, we all drifted away
as soon as we could . . . when I came back to Lowestoft
I took my wife down to show her where I was brought up
and couldn't believe it . . . Birds Eye and all the neat
business premises now, and I couldn't even find where I lived
in Anguish Street, it was all gone . . ."*

E. J. DAY

"It could have been a wonderfully pretty little place down here still," the late Bob 'Umshi' Norman told the Eastern Evening News in September 1966. "I shall be glad to get away now . . . Everywhere is smashed up and no-one does a thing about it."

The Beach Village had become a ghost town, with only a few people living amongst the tumbledown streets and derelict houses. 'Slum clearance' had gone on for some time but in the 1960s this process was accelerated, in a new optimistic era which sought to sweep away much of the old. At this time the Beach Village seemed to represent a grim, dark, depressing age of hardship and poverty and in 1964 was described as "a relic of less prosperous days" by the Eastern Daily Press. The end was perhaps best symbolised by the demolition of the last two long-serving public houses, the *Gas House Tavern*, demolished in October 1967 with the *Rising Sun* following soon after, with its last memorable night on the 4th November 1968, when the place was drunk dry. By the beginning of the 1970s there was little to remind anyone of the huddle of cottages and houses and narrow streets which had been home to 2500 people in 1900, and significantly more every autumn when the Scots arrived for the herring season. At that time the strong feeling of independence among the Gritsters was understandable – there was no need to venture up into the town – as every shop and service was available within this community, in addition to thirteen pubs! The Beach was even an ecclesiastical parish, with its own church in addition to a chapel. The residents worked there too, the men mostly as fishermen while many of the women worked in the net stores or mended the fishing nets at home. There were smoke houses, rope and twine-spinning sheds, all related to a booming fishing industry but the crews and labourers were never well paid, although the hardship was shared and a strong community emerged.

The demise of the Beach Village had set in by the 1930s. The slump of the fishing industry, in addition to the general economic depression of this period, caused further privation to the Beach between the wars and in some cases the living conditions of these people were terrible. An example of the worst of these dwellings is given in a 1933 inquiry into a clearance order on four houses in Anguish Street. One of these properties, said to be typical of the rest, was stated as being poorly built and laid out and now had "crumbling walls and a leaking roof . . .". The rear of the house was overshadowed by a factory and ". . . the living room and one of the bedrooms was in a perpetual state of semi-darkness with no window ventilation and two of the bedrooms had ceilings that sloped down to just over four feet. The scullery floor was over six inches below street level and there was one tap with no sink, the water dripping on to the brick floor."

In defence, the owner of this property pointed out that the tenant of the house had lived in it for thirty-three years and raised a family of eleven and suggested improvements could be made with the demolition of the rear of the house and the erection of a lean-to kitchen. However, the Borough Surveyor, Mr Mobbs, fiercely disagreed saying the house was unfit for habitation and he would not keep a dog in the living room! The clearance order went ahead and the tenants were rehoused.

Unfortunately, the fashion for modernisation came about fifty years too late for the Beach, as in the early 1930s the Town Council began a scheme of slum clearance in the area, with the idea of building a council estate in its place. In September 1937 the Lowestoft Corporation Redevelopment Scheme started and ended in Lighthouse Score, with new council houses being built to replace the picturesque old cottages which were still occupied. The Second World War however thwarted any further redevelopment plans.

The Beach found itself on the front line and some families were evacuated from the town and part of the Beach became uninhabited. The army used these deserted streets and houses to train allied soldiers in the techniques of house-to-house fighting. The north beach was sealed off, and became an immense minefield as a result of which the sea wall was off-limits. However, not everyone appreciated these dangers, and on one occasion, having heard that a cargo boat had been sunk off Lowestoft and that a load of butter had been washed up on the beach, Ronny 'Titch' Wilson, Jack Rose and John Wooley decided to look for it. Finding a gap in the barbed wire, they walked onto the Denes and made their way to the sea wall. About half way across they heard someone shouting and looking back saw a man in a peaked cap, together with three or four sailors, all waving their arms about. Ignoring them, they carried on to the beach but found nothing there. On the way back they met the man and the sailors who collared the three boys and told them that they had just walked through a minefield!

"We left the Beach when I was seven in 1940," says Danny Burwood who lived at 65 East Street, " as my mother was frightened of the gasworks being hit. We were within a hundred yards of it and there would have been an almighty explosion." The Germans certainly did target the gasworks, and there were many air raids in this area. Joy Pearce lived in Rant Score East but she could see an advantage in living so close to this target, "It was handy living right near to the gasworks because we used to be able to hear their crash warning, which was a three minute warning before enemy planes came over, a little bit before the normal sirens so we could get in the shelter first." Thankfully, the gasworks were never directly hit, but the near misses did turn many surrounding properties into ruins. "We suffered structural damage," Mrs Pearce continues. "I was up with some friends in Reeve Street in the town, my grandfather was in the merchant navy but my grandmother was at home and the ceilings came down. We had to move out and took most of the stuff up to Camden

Street in a tin bath, while the heavy stuff was moved by Hailey's."

'Bimbo' Osborne lived at 18 Rant Score East next to Binks' Bakery. His house was bombed in 1941 and the two people next door were killed. He recalled, "My brother worked at the gasworks and saw the bomb drop just off the gas holder and ran to his house to get his wife out."

Looking down Rant Score East, towards the gasworks. The gap at the end of these row of houses on the left is where a bomb fell during the Second World War, showing how close the gasworks came to being hit. The end two houses were occupied by the Jensens and the Turrells, while at No. 3 were the Cullums.

Sadly, there were casualties. Sonny Smith recalls, "I was near Binks the bakers when they tried to hit the gasworks, and the blast blew this baby right out of the pram, and it landed on the railings, it was hanging there, so I picked it off and all the brains fell out . . ."

On 3rd May 1941 the blast of a parachute mine which fell on the sea wall caused structural damage to four hundred and fifty houses. Wilde's School building which was being used as the Headquarters of the Lowestoft Air Training Corps was also struck and, more tragically, on 13th June 1941 two bombs hit the Central School where soldiers had been sleeping, killing fourteen and injuring six. "I was digging the bodies out of Central School after that got hit," recalls Ronny Wilson. "My

On 20th August, 1941 eight high-explosives fell on East Street, Nelson Road and Fishery Street. This picture shows one of the bomb craters in East Street which destroyed a blockhouse with a machine gun post. The two houses on the right were 65 East Street, where the Burwoods lived next door to the Crittens at 67. In the centre of the photograph can be seen Burwood's fish house and beyond that, out of camera shot, was the North Beach Bethel.

father and I went round. We were digging them out about three o'clock in the morning. They were all soldiers down there but they left the lights on. I think they got a direct hit and one of them we found right up in the High Street."

Photograph showing the bomb damage to the interior of the hall at Central School, where 14 soldiers and 1 civilian were killed, and another 6 people were injured.

"Our Anderson shelter was opposite the Little Bethel," recalls Jean Mitchell (née Keable). "During the heavy air-raids we used to run from our house in Wilde's Street to the shelter in East Street. When it got really bad we practically lived in the shelter. My Mum used to cook potatoes and boil kettles on a round oil heater. This caused condensation where the water ran down the metal frame of the shelter making the bed we slept in very, very damp . . ."

Many families never returned to the Beach after the Second World War, and were rehoused in the new post-war council estates. With new industries being encouraged into this area after 1946 there was no attempt made to renovate or repair any of the houses. However, the ensuing housing shortage delayed any immediate redevelopment, and new residents moved onto the 'Grit' attracted by cheaper accommodation, and in some cases lived there for up to twenty years. The arrival of Birds Eye Foods to this area in 1949 would also prove to be a significant factor. Originally just a small depot opened for the preparation and packaging of fruit for the Great Yarmouth factory, but subsequently the Lowestoft operation went from strength to strength, and expanded over much of the site of the old Beach Village.

The war had caused untold damage to the Grit, both structural and to the community itself, although perhaps the most immediate problem was the sea wall. Prior to the war it had been supported on the landward side by sand hills covered in marram grass but these disappeared during the occupation by the naval and military authorities and it was feared that the sea wall might collapse.

Gradually the sea did undermine the wall and on 23rd March 1946 the Eastern Evening News reported, "Lowestoft Wall Breached . . . A change in direction of the wind on Sunday brought relief to those who had been anxiously watching at the north sea wall since Saturday . . . Flooding has been averted but extensive undermining was revealed . . . On Saturday the officials who visited the scene, Mr G. A. M. Gentry, Borough Engineer, and Mr S. W. Mobbs, Engineer to the East Norfolk Rivers Catchment Board, who was surveyor when the wall was built, were concerned with the safety of the 6ft. flood wall, which if breached, would have caused serious flooding of the Denes, possibly involving the gasworks and business and residential property . . . As Mr Mobbs points out, the continual pounding of any defences will find the weak spots, and if not attended to immediately there is no limit to the amount of damage which might follow. That is what has happened to this wall; for six years the sea has had free play, because maintenance work could not be carried out . . . Thousands of tons of sand have been scooped from beneath the wall as if it had been tunnelled, hence the collapse of 300 feet of the decking some 40 feet wide. The subsidence is anything up to six feet . . ."

Although the sea wall was patched up to prevent any immediate breaching by the sea, the faults in the structure were irreparable and it became obvious that a new one needed to be built. Mr Gentry was given the task of designing another sea wall,

In March 1946 the Mobbs' sea wall finally collapsed as the result of a strong north east wind. The wall had fallen into a state of disrepair during the Second World War and was found to be seriously undermined. Although the wall was patched up, a new one was hastily designed by Mr Gentry and building work soon began. The photograph shows how far work had progressed in April 1947.

which was 11ft. 3ins. high and 6 ft. wide with 18 groynes extending into the sea at intervals and it is this wall that still protects the area today.

Many of the villagers had experienced flooding by the time the 1953 surge occurred. "Normally flood water came through the drains," remembers Matthew Boardley, who lived at 1 Jubilee Terrace on Whapload Road. "The tide would come up and it would all go through the drains and we'd get flooded. My mother would send me out to see if the water was coming up through the drain, and as soon as it did I had to run in and tell her so she could put the flood-boards up. The 1953 flood was different though, a wall of water swept down Whapload Road."

It was the most disastrous flood the east coast had ever seen. A new record high tide of twenty-six feet split Lowestoft and Oulton Broad in two. The Beach Village was the worst affected area, the low lying streets soon waist deep, and the water-level on the pickling plots and the net drying ground soon rose to four or five feet. With other men of the village Mr Gus Jensen, the then licensee of the *Rising Sun*, made a round of all the houses to warn occupants and kept an all-night patrol with Willie Boothroyd and Dan Dyer, waist deep in a current of water that kept knocking them off their feet. Indeed, it was for this brave night's work that Gus received the British Empire Medal.

The Tucks lived in Wilde's Street where the water came up as high as 3ft. 3ins. in the house, "I remember them coming and measuring it afterwards by the water marks on the walls," says Beryl Clover (née Tuck). That night her mother was in the *Gas House Tavern*, while sister Norma was in the house with her other sister and her boyfriend. "As mother got home the water was gurgling in the drains," recalls Norma. "To me, as a child, that was exciting. I remember looking out of the window and seeing things floating past, but I wasn't at an age when it worried me. We were getting the furniture up, putting the settee on the table, and the chairs upside down on the settee and as we were trying to do this, the water started coming in the door. So we went upstairs. We stayed up all night. Father had chickens outside in the shed and he went out and opened it up so they could get on the roof or something high but I think we still lost four."

Beryl continues, "We had a little fireplace upstairs which we were trying to keep alight next day to dry off things that were wet downstairs. There was nothing you could do, the whole area was mud outside, you couldn't put anything on the line, it was just mud, so everything had to be dried inside."

John Day lived at 2 Canary Cottages, Whapload Road and was ten years old when the 1953 flood occurred. "The night was very angry with screaming winds, and in the early morning lots of dead horses and pigs were found not far from our house. My father knew one of the coastguards, and we went to see him at the little look-out near Hamilton Dock. Everywhere was covered in thick, gooey, sticky, clinging, stinking mud and we saw more dead animals."

Colin Dixon recalls, "During the 1953 flood my grandfather was at sea and whenever he was at sea, my grandmother came and stayed with us, and by that time we had moved up to St. Peter's Street to Sparham's Buildings. When grandmother went to go home this particular Sunday, she met her milkman who asked where she was going. She said, 'I'm going home,' and he replied, 'You'll never get down there, Kate, it's been flooded!' So she came back home and we all went down into the Beach Village."

"I was eleven at the time, and when we reached the road down there, there was still water. Grandma was worried about the contents of the sideboard, where she kept some money, so a neighbour waded with me on his back, from Maltsters Score through Salter Street and we went into Wilde's Street, into the house, opened up, got into the sideboard, got the things we wanted and then went back. Everything was topsy-turvy, all the furniture had been thrown about by the water. After the flood, she did go back to live there though. The family all got together, in those days they did, and everybody rallied round, and they went into Grandma's house, stripped everything out, washed and scraped off all the mud, and she went back to live there for a number of years."

Joan Reynolds moved to Whapload Road a year before the flood on 6th February 1952, which was the day King George VI died. She recalls, ". . . I lived there with my husband Jack and our two little lads, Christopher and Paul. As I remember it, the actual day of the flood was very, very windy, there was a strange atmosphere, it was really a peculiar sort of day." Jack was at work that night and Joan thankfully managed to scramble to safety with her children up the cliff. ". . . Next morning, Jack put on some high waders and managed to get through to the house," Joan continues. "He wanted to retrieve money and personal items before any looting started, which did happen. I didn't go back for quite a while though."

"When I did go back there was still water in the kitchen. When you think of it, I had the sea in my house! There had been about five foot of water and the damage was horrendous. It was like a wet bombing raid. The front door had gone, the garden wall had gone, the front windows had been smashed. I had other people's furniture in my house, my own furniture had been swept away and disappeared. The sideboard had been turned on its side and smashed on the floor. We had mostly lino then but where the sea had swirled round that had all been churned up into little fragments. The joint of beef we had been going to have on the Sunday was still in the kitchen, bobbing about in the water, and the knitting was still on the table with one ball of wool hanging in the water, turned all black. They had to knock a hole in the wall to drain the water out of there. We lost so much that couldn't be replaced, like our wedding photographs."

"We lived with my mother for three weeks until we came back and lived upstairs. The RAF came along and helped us to dry out, we had food parcels and a carpet from Canada, there was a Lord Mayor's fund which gave us a little bit of money, but we had no insurance. We got it all together again though and lived there for another ten years."

The 1953 flood proved to be a huge blow to the Beach Village, causing many people and businesses to leave the area for good. "Within six months of the flood we were out of the *Kumfy Kafe*," remembers Ron James. "We had just opened a fish and chip shop the night before, next to our *Kumfy Kafe*, and it was only open one night!" His wife Doris recalls, "We'd paid for all the pans in the fish and chip shop and of course, when we got up next morning, all the pans were full of water but no fish in it! They were ruined. We were very lucky though really. We were the only business down there that was insured for sea flood and the only reason we were was because the Prudential agent pointed it out to us, 'Do you want to be insured for sea flood?' he said. 'If you don't specifically state it, you won't get it,' and it cost another half a crown a year. So he put it down and so luckily we were covered. We were flooded out on the Saturday night and the Prudential were knocking at the door on Monday morning with an open cheque. They were very good to us."

"The only thing that wasn't covered was the car, a little Austin 7. I could just get this Austin 7 into an Anderson shelter, which I used as a garage, and of course,

Drying out the laundry boxes in front of the Steam Laundry building after the floods of 1953. All the buildings to the right of the photograph have been demolished.

East Street, after the water abated the following day. The logs in the picture had been stacked near the pickling plots and were swept around the Beach Village by the sea, ramming against many of the properties although fortunately causing no serious damage.

when the water came along it lifted the bloody thing up and we couldn't get the car out. Of course, we did get it out eventually, and the seats were floating inside and were jammed into the roof. We got compensation from the flood fund for that though."

Those that did stay tried to get on with their lives in the ailing village. Jean Mitchell lived at 19 Wilde's Street. She recalls, "When the water subsided it left behind filthy sludge, very smelly. All my Mum's furniture was ruined, it took many weeks to get some order back and many months to get everywhere clean. We didn't have trauma clinics then. You all had to get stuck in, pull yourselves together and and get on with life."

Property was damaged, belongings lost, and people, fearful of another North Sea surge with fatal consequences, were rehoused in the town. The flood certainly hastened the demise of the Beach, and in 1955 the local press announced details of the 'First Stage of Slum Clearance Programme' which included the whole area east of Whapload Road from Marsh Cottage in the north to the Bath House at the corner of Hamilton Road. Familiar buildings and roads were now disappearing and existing streets, like East Street, Spurgeon Street and Fishery Street, became over-shadowed by the growing Birds Eye Food factory. In the early 1960s the residents remaining began to drift away, houses were boarded up, and some derelict properties became the haunts of winos and unsavoury characters. The area was run-down and in a sorry state, with the Chief Public Health Inspector, a Mr Cormack, commenting at the time that ". . . the Beach Village does not even possess a veneer of olde worlde charm."

The Beach was doomed, and in these last days many old Gritsters took one last sentimental walk round these derelict streets. "See that little house over there," 'Umshi' Norman recalled to a reporter in 1966. "A family of seven boys and a girl were brought up there. Only two bedrooms, they were a lovely family . . . It was a real community down here when I was boy."

With smashed windows and doors off their hinges, Anguish Street had been allowed to fall into a dilapidated condition by the late 1960s.

The last days of the Beach Village, looking north down Whapload Road from the area of Christ Church, in the late 1960s. All the buildings to the right of the photograph were soon to be swept away.

A boarded up Nelson Road leading to the Princess Royal public house which can be seen at the far end of this street, in the centre of the photograph. Beyond that is A. & S. Boardley's yard.

The same area seen from East Street, with A. & S. Boardley's yard on the centre right. The Princess Royal has been demolished and the site of the pub can be seen on the left.

The clearance of the site for Day's Garage at the south end of Whapload Road was well under way by the time this photograph was taken in 1971. On the right can be seen the three gas holders, two of which would also be demolished four years later. On the left is Christ Church, the mainstay of the Beach Village, which is still there to this day.

Looking south from Gasworks Road in the late 1960s. On the right can be seen derelict property at the east end of Wilde Street.

2

'The Town Below the Cliff'

"The 'Beach' area had an old world charm all its own . . .
many of the cottages were flint-faced and had pantile roofs
of that warm red shade of the days gone by . . ."

HUGH LEES

It was in 1791 that the first primitive houses were built on the Denes, to the east of the town. Edmund Gillingwater records that seventy-six tenements were erected here over the next fifteen years, which was the birth of what we know as the Beach Village, or simply the Beach, a town below the cliff. At first these dwellings were outnumbered by the many fish houses which were located in this area. A guide book from 1812 records that at the bottom of the cliff these buildings were so numerous that ". . . had they been built more compactly, they would have been sufficient to form a small town of themselves . . ." but a small town was exactly what would evolve over the course of that century.

All of the Denes were privately owned and permission to build on the Beach had to be obtained from the Lord of the Manor, as the whole of this site was considered to be his waste land. The Corporation bought the manorial rights to the Denes in 1889, but originally strict conditions were applied to these buildings, which could not exceed a certain height and rent was due from those occupying the land. An example of this comes to light in various deeds from the early 1800s concerning Matthew Colman, who had to obtain such a licence from the Lord of the Manor to build Ethel Cottage which stood at 1 Nelson Road, known as Nelson Score East at the time.

Ethel Cottage was still standing and in use after the Second World War, "My father was Charles Hall and he was born down there. He lived near Christ Church in Ethel Cottage," recalls Joan Hall. "I think there were five brothers and six sisters all in this two bedroom house."

The fishing industry was responsible for the growth of the Beach Village. This had always been an obvious area for such activities, and fish houses could be found along the base of the cliff in the sixteenth century. In the mid-seventeeth century cod livers were boiled on the Denes in large iron coppers to extract the oil and when Lowestoft became involved with whaling later that same century, it was here they boiled the blubber for the oil. The decline of the Dutch fleet and the end of the Napoleonic wars in 1815 freed the North Sea for our own fishing operation. "Before the harbour was made the beach was busier than now," comments Arthur Stebbings in his Guidebook to Lowestoft in 1886. "The fish were all brought ashore and sold on the beach, and great indeed was the stir." The harbour, built in 1831,

The north beach, Lowestoft, 1860.

Loading fish on the north beach before the pier heads or harbour were built.

wasn't a success initially until it was acquired by Samuel Morton Peto, who developed it alongside a railway in the 1840s, and its full potential was achieved. Now the fishing industry began to expand, causing more houses to be built with a pattern of streets forming. In early documents this area is referred to as the 'Beach Village' but by the late nineteenth century it was known to the locals as the 'Beach' or the 'Grit'.

Leading down from the High Street to the Beach Village were the twelve 'Scores', which are unique to Lowestoft. Many of the 'Beach' families would live in these scores, all of which are believed to have had ancient origins, and were no doubt formed over a period of many years, with footsteps wearing paths into the soft, sloping cliffs to the Beach, and tracks were eventually formed with steps added to a few. Although the exact origin of the word 'score' is unknown, it is thought that it could be a corruption of 'scour', or possibly from the Old English 'scora', related to the Norse 'skor' which means to make or cut a line. The condition of the road surfaces in the scores was notoriously poor and in winter months would be dangerous and sometimes impassable. The steps were irregular too, in those scores that had them, and were usually beside flowing open drains.

Many of the scores took their names from the people or the public houses which could be found in their locality although Mariners Score would seem to be an exception to this. Names were frequently changed over the centuries and sometimes scores were known by more than one name. The street names on the Beach were no doubt derived in much the same way, but it wasn't until the 1860s that they were officially given names. In a meeting of the Lowestoft Improvement Commissioners in 1863 the names for streets on the east side of Whapload Road were suggested by the Paving Committee. They were Rant Score East, Anquish Street, Wilde's Score East (later known as Wilde's Street), Cumberland Square, Nelson Road, Coleman Square and Neave Court, which may have been an earlier name for Barcham Square. Anquish Street is believed to have been named after the Rev. George Anquish, who was the Lord of the Manor, living at Somerleyton Hall before Sir Samuel Morton Peto. Over the years this road name was sometimes corrupted to Anguish Street, which is how it appeared on the street signs, but remained Anquish Street on some maps. The inconsistent nature of street names on the Beach is again illustrated by Hazel Boardley (née Disney). Hazel says, "I lived opposite the *Rising Sun*. Our house had two numbers, 56 Whapload Road and 1 Spurgeon Street, as we had doors on both roads, so that was all a bit confusing!"

As the Beach Village grew so the fishing fleet continued to expand, but prior to the arrival of Kentish men in 1860, who brought trawling to the town, the fleet consisted entirely of drifters. By the end of the next decade the number of trawlers had risen to a hundred and eleven, and accounted for thirty per cent of the fleet. However, few of these fishermen from Ramsgate and Kent settled on the Beach as the majority of them were either skippers or masters and could afford to live in other parts of the town, many of them in Denmark Road and Clapham Road. In the 1880s, as many of the local skippers who lived on the Beach became prosperous, they also moved into the town to new houses which were being built in Worthing Road and Sussex Road, which became known as the 'Skipper Rows'. The 1860s also saw the arrival of the first Scottish vessels to visit Lowestoft. Originally these were just from the Firth of Forth, but by the 1890s the fleet had grown to an invasion from Scotland's east coast. The Scots brought their womenfolk down too, arriving on special trains, and their job was to gut the fish, which they did with stunning dexterity. More of the Scots settled here than the Kentish trawlermen, and many of the Beach people we spoke to in the course of writing this book had Scottish connections. A fish market was opened in 1872 to cope with the influx of the Scottish fleet as there simply hadn't been enough room at existing quays for both trading vessels and fishing boats and it was becoming increasingly inconvenient for larger craft who were still landing their catches on the north beach.

The Denes were purchased by the Corporation in September 1889 for around £2,500 from the trustees of the last Lord of the Manor, Mr Richard Henry Reeve, who had died in 1888. Many plans were subsequently put forward concerning the use of this land, and in 1897 a possible route was proposed for a railway line between Yarmouth and Lowestoft which cut straight through the Denes, and although the Council were in favour of the idea, there were many protests from the public and the idea came to nothing. Around the same time there were proposals for a pier to be built opposite Lighthouse Score, and in 1897, the Duke of Cambridge visited the town for the purpose of cutting the first turf for this structure. This was to be part of a larger scheme which would involve a winding road from the High Street to Whapload Road, and a fine approach road to the pier wide enough for trams, and was to be flanked by shops and restaurants. There would be three ornate gateways, the third leading to the pier itself, and situated at the end of this would be a grand entertainment hall, holding 2,000 people. This was to cost £60,000 but after the initial ceremony nothing happened and although the North Pier was referred to at a few subsequent Council meetings nothing was done and the project sank without trace.

Throughout history, the Denes have been utilised in many ways. There has been a long tradition of fairs held on this area below the cliff dating back to the fifteenth century. Centuries later, Old Spillings Fair was held around Easter on the site which would become the pickling plots. This was before the First World War, and was originally known as Pilling's fair but over the years the name became corrupted. The original Pilling was a police sergeant and he was responsible for choosing the site after an application was made to hold a fair in the town. In April 1887 it is recorded that a fair was held on the Denes, which attracted a considerable number of visitors and the roundabouts and other similar attractions proved popular with the youngsters. However, it is said that one of the showmen lost a valuable horse when it fell and was drowned in the Warren Pond which was situated near to Warren House.

At the north end of Whapload Road was the summer home and park of the Sparrow family, Robert Sparrow being a co-founder with Rev. Francis Bowness of the Lowestoft lifeboat at the beginning of the 19th century. The estate, which also included two fish houses and the fishermen's cottages in Lighthouse Score, was known as Sparrow's Nest and in 1897 it was bought by the Corporation for over £11,000 and the following year was let to Frank Stebbings, the High Street printer, who erected a stage in the grounds where he presented a circus and variety show. In July 1913 the Sparrow's Nest Theatre was erected in the gardens which by that time had become a public park.

The Denes were also the site where the town's football and cricket teams originally played. The cricket ground was built at the seaward end of a ropewalk, with a pavilion that stood opposite Lighthouse Score. Around the area was dug a deep ditch to prevent vehicular traffic and stray horses and cattle encroaching on it. A yacht pond was built on the Denes and opened in July 1889 by the Mayor, with model yachts and yawls sailing here in the summer. During the winter, when the water was frozen, it was used for skating and fancy dress carnivals, the area being illuminated by coloured lanterns. In August 1919 large marquees were set up on the North Denes for a 'welcome home' feast given to the 3,500 soldiers and sailors returning from the First World War. Liquid refreshments included 30 barrels of beer and 115 gallons of mineral water. Afterwards they were joined by their womenfolk for an entertainment at Sparrow's Nest. The sporting activities on the Denes continued into the twentieth century, with the Denes Oval laid out in 1925 on land that had been allotments for at least sixty years, and included a cricket pitch and tennis courts. A year later saw the establishment of the Corton Golf Club, who laid out their course, partly on the Denes and partly on the cliff top. A swimming pool was built on the Denes and opened on the 7th July 1921. This open-air pool contained water pumped direct from the sea and was 150 feet long by 100 feet wide with a depth of water varying from three feet to six feet. There was also a diving board and a water chute and was in use until the Second World War when it received bomb damage and was subsequently filled in. The swimming pool was near the site where once rifle butts had been situated and used by the local Volunteers for their musketry practice. This was also where the Artillery Volunteers used to fire at floating targets far out to sea.

Until the Second World War, the north beach was as popular as the south beach for bathing, and there was evidence of the increasing popularity of the seaside holiday in the nineteenth century even in a fishing area such as the Beach Village. From the early 1800s there was a Bath House on the Beach where bathers were provided with heated sea-water. By 1824 it was deemed necessary to build a new Bath House which was larger and offered more facilities, such as 'sulphureous medicated baths', and was run by 'four gentlemen' who sold it to a Mr Walter Jones in 1830. The advertisements of the day made it plain that the baths would operate

A new Bath House was built on the Beach in 1824 by four gentlemen who sold it in 1830 to Mr Walter Jones, although hot and cold baths were established on this site many years before by a Mr Wells. White's Suffolk of 1844 says of the new Bath House, ". . . It is an oblong building with rusticated angles and has a spacious reading room, and hot and cold baths . . ." Although not in use for some time the building remained much the same until it was pulled down in the late 1960s, standing as it did on the southern boundary of the Beach demolition area.

only during the summer season and it seems likely they were built for the summer visitors rather than locals. By 1884 the Bath House had passed into the hands of the Cook family, who had had a long association with this area, letting bathing machines from the north beach since 1768. In 1901 there was an attempt to convert the Bath House into a hotel, joining it with two other nearby properties, Kent House and Beach House. The scheme would have cost £9,000 and was put forward by Frank Stanley Dorling who applied for an order to move the full licence of the *Albion Stores* in the High Street to the new hotel. The local magistrates refused and the plans were scrapped.

The early 1900s saw the building of the first of the three sea walls in this area. Although all of these structures have been inundated by the North Sea they have been invaluable, if only to provide a breakwater for the force of the water which, had there not been a sea wall in place, would have proved devastating on a number of occasions. On November 26th 1925 Mobb's wall faced a record high tide of 24 feet and the whole of the Beach Village was flooded to a depth of about two feet and thousands of herring barrels were washed through the streets. In all, two hundred and fifty houses were flooded, some to a depth of three feet. It seems likely that this is the occasion that Ruby Timberley (née Dalley) remembers, "I was about six years old, attending Mariners Score School. I think it was in the early afternoon, when a man came round ringing a bell and telling mothers to collect their children from Mariners Score School and get them upstairs, and our mother came along with other mothers to collect us. The sight will remain with me always of when I looked out of the bedroom window to see fish barrels floating in Anguish Street with driftwood and seaweed. The sea was very deep and was splashing against the walls of the houses and coming indoors to about three feet high. We children were terrified. I think the adults were too. Of course, everywhere was soaked in sea water. Gradually the tide turned and the sea went back. The council of the day allowed each householder 1 cwt. (a hundredweight) of coal free to help dry out."

The area below the cliff had frequently suffered from flooding, and Gillingwater recorded that in the early 1700s if a spring tide coincided with a north-west gale, the sea would force its way over the beach and sweep across the Denes, into the fish-houses and approach the hanging gardens, which were the back gardens of properties in the High Street which ran down to the bottom of the cliff. Over the centuries the sandbanks, which once acted as breakwaters, diminished and the sea gradually encroached. The evidence of this erosion is recorded by Edmund Gillingwater in 1790, who states that at the time he was writing his book, *Gillingwater's History of Lowestoft*, there were at least three fathoms of water over an area which had been dry land in the reign of Henry VIII. At the beginning of the following century there were still visible sandbanks, as after the Battle of Waterloo in 1815 an effigy of Napoleon was placed there and by 1861 Beachmen even used to run trips to Holm Sands, where on one occasion a cricket match was played. There had been a lengthy beach beyond Ness Point where you could find the Marram Hills, named after the marram grass which grew there and held together the sand which was being gradually washed away.

A flood in November 1897 must have served as a warning to the Council who subsequently began to consider the erection of a substantial wooden wall along the sea front, running a distance of eighteen hundred yards, from Ness Point to the boundary of Mr Coleman's estate at Corton. The lowest tender for this work was £6,900 but the council decided to consult an expert in these matters, a Mr Douglas, who charged 30 guineas for his consultation which consisted of two visits to the site before he drew up a plan and quoted £34,356 to carry out the work. The main part of his scheme was the construction of a concrete retaining wall, at a cost of £10,500, which would run the whole length of the front to the Ness. Mr Douglas maintained that the wall would keep the sea from flooding the Denes, and that the groynes would prevent the encroachment which had been so marked during the previous ten years. The committee were not satisfied with this at first, as a concrete wall of the length he proposed seemed a rather substantial affair and they deferred their decision for further discussion but eventually the plan was accepted and the Douglas Wall was built in 1902–3 which withstood the pounding of the North Sea until the early 1920s.

In 1922 a new sea wall was constructed. Designed by Mr S. W. Mobbs, this included a roadway which became a popular promenade. A bus service ran along here in the summer, giving the seasonal visitors a closer look at the Beach Village. In 1927 this roadway was also used for both car and motor cyle racing, with a mile long course laid out, with tuning pits which were situated on a site which later became the corporation depot. On one occasion a magnificent cup was donated by the town council and a crowd estimated at 6,000 saw the cars and motor cycles hurtling along the sea wall. It is said that one racing car reached a speed of 100 mph in the days when lorry drivers were being fined for exceeding the 12 mph speed limit in the town!

In September 1927 the decking on the new sea wall was completed and almost immediately used for motor cycle and car speed trials, shown in the photograph. The sixty foot wide decking, a mile and a half long, was declared ideal for such trials. It was never held again, though the following year motor cycles raced round the gravel perimeter of Normanston Park.

The sea wall was again where many people gathered on the 7th June 1931, when Lowestoft suffered an earthquake. It was felt that the vibrations had come from the sea and there were fears that the fishing trawlers could be damaged and there followed an anxious wait before they all returned safely to harbour. Although there was no serious damage, the quake did do some. George Wilson, who lived on Whapload Road recalls, "During the earthquake in the 1930s our chimney fell off and dropped on our shed!"

The old lighthouse over-looking the beginnings of the 'town under the cliff' in the first half of the eighteenth century. In 1829 John Kirby noted in his Topographical and Historical Description of the County of Suffolk, "... At the bottom of the (hanging) gardens ... there is a long range of building erected for the purpose of curing fish, extending the whole length of the town, which from its distance from the spot where this operation is performed, escapes the disagreeable effluvia arising from the herrings whilst under cure ..."

3

The Beachmen

". . . Everyone took an interest in the Beach Companies
in those days, and the almost deserted Beach
was soon all alive when the cry
of 'Running Down' was heard . . ."

LETTER TO THE LOWESTOFT JOURNAL, 6TH FEBRUARY 1897

"When one strolls on the beach," writes Arthur Stebbings in his Guidebook to
Lowestoft in 1886, "the beachmen may be remarked by their absence, for look
where you will not one is to be seen, do not imagine they are not at hand, they are
like the warriors of Roderick Dhu, numerous though not seen; let a ship strike the
sands or come ashore, and out of the cavernous depths of the 'shods' they pour in
goodly numbers, equal to any emergency and ready for any deed of rescue. The
visitors do not often witness these scenes for they come in fair sunny weather . . ."

The Beachmen were fishermen, supplementing their income with salvage work,
assisting the sailing ships which ran into trouble off the coast. They also picked up
work carrying fish to markets in London in addition to taking the pilots from the
shore to ships which required guidance coming into the harbour.

Jack Rose was born in 1926, and when he was a child his grandfather used to take
him to the Young Company shed, or 'shod' as the fishermen called it, near the gasworks. This old building seemed to be held together with tar, and was adorned with
old ships' figure-heads and name plates from wrecks. To a young boy though, it
seemed dark and spooky with a strong smell of salt, tar and sweat. This was the
headquarters of the Young Company, who in earlier days had played a prominent
part in life at sea.

In 1886 Arthur Stebbings commented on the shods in the Guidebook to
Lowestoft, writing that they were, ". . . Well furnished with sails, spars, ropes,
excellent though odd-looking telescopes, through which the beachmen do not look
into the middle of next week exactly, but by which they know that a ship is on the
sands before the ship's crew know it and they launch their gigs and are half-way to
the rescue before the crew know in what jeopardy they are. These sheds are painted
with the gayest of colours, and the figureheads of vessels whose crews have been
saved are displayed thereon . . ."

In the nineteenth century there were three Companies in Lowestoft and whenever
a ship was spotted in distress the yawls would be launched from the shore and there
was a frantic race, with the first yawl to make contact with the endangered vessel
being rewarded with the job according to the laws of salvage. There was money to
be made from salvaging, and as a result, there was no shortage of assistance for

(Left):

The Old Company shod with Brock Ellis holding the telescope, and standing to his left, 'Sheppey' Hook.

(Below):

Situated near to the gasworks, the Young Company shod is remembered for having a small cannon outside, which is shown in this photograph taken in the 1920s.

troubled vessels. In the early days the Beachmen were also linked with smuggling and had a notorious reputation, with some considering them nothing more than scavengers, branding them 'longshore sharks and pirates'. However, the Beachmen saved many lives from stricken vessels, and they were needed, especially in the days before lifeboat stations and harbour tugs which would, in time, gradually take over the Beachmen's role. Lowestoft's first lifeboat was established in 1801, built by Henry Greathead at Shields for £105. The Beachmen were obvious choices for the lifeboat crew but they refused to use her, claiming she was unsuitable to this particular part of the coast. After much discussion a replacement boat, *Frances Ann* was built in 1807 for £200 by Barcham, who had his yard in the Beach Village. This vessel, built by a local ship builder, was obviously preferred and served until 1859, saving three hundred lives during that period.

The Beachmen continued to combine manning the lifeboat in addition to their salvage work and, in many cases, fishing activities. However, by the time Jack Rose was a child in the 1930s, the Company shods had evolved into little more than club-rooms for the lifeboatmen. During the Second World War the two remaining historic 'shods' were used by the military and both suffered bomb damage and all the old pictures, name-plates and figure-heads were taken away. After the war, compensation was received for the damage to the Beach Company property and a Nissen hut was erected near the sea wall, to the north of the coastguard look-out. This was called the 'The Lowestoft Lifeboat and Life Saving Apparatus Social Club' and subsequently moved to the former Ayers' net store in East Street and then to premises at the end of Hamilton Road in 1962 before the lifeboat crew broke away and formed the 'Lowestoft Lifeboatmen's Crewman's Association'. These clubs are the last link with the Beachmen and their Companies.

The earliest mention of any Lowestoft Beach Company is in 1762, with references to Companies run by two brothers, Thomas and Nicholas Martin and another owned by John Masterson. This was followed by the arrival of three new Beach Companies in the 1780s to cope with the increase in salvage and pilotage work. Denny's, Reed's and Lincoln's were owned by private individuals, pilots who were also publicans in the cases of Joseph Denny and William Lincoln. Originally Beachmen merely crewed the boats but in 1835 the pilots left and the Companies were all reorganised, the Beachmen buying shares in the boats. The oldest, Denny's Company, which was by then known as 'Denny's Old', was now re-named the Old Company, while Reed's and Lincoln's amalgamated and became known as the New or Young Company. A third, the North Roads Company, named after the area where it principally fished, is believed to have been established in 1837 although some sources claim that the date was 1845. Each had around sixty to eighty members and any man who wanted to become a member had to purchase a share of the yawls, have his name entered in the books and he was then entitled to work the boats and form one of the lifeboat crew. Widows were allowed to put a man into the boats to work the shares owned by their late husbands or be looked after in some other way. The younger men would only take half a dole until they reached a certain age. A veteran Beachman was appointed to look after the sails, gear and shed and another member looked after the financial side of the Company, keeping the books and paying all the bills for repair. With money at stake, the rivalry between each Company was intense, and although the Old and Young Companies joined up in the 1850s and formed the United Beach Company the partnership was short-lived and they soon returned to their separate identities.

The Beachmen would receive their wages or 'doles' in one of the public houses. The Lowestoft Beach Companies had their own pubs dating back to the days when Joseph Denny owned the *Herring Fishery* and William Lincoln owned the *Jolly Maltsters* next to Maltsters Score. The North Roads Company had the *George and Dragon* which from 1850 to 1875 became known as the *Norwich Arms* in the High Street.

Each Company had two or three yawls, and one of the smaller vessels, called gigs, which were used in calmer weather. The yawls were tarred originally, but over the years were painted instead. At first, their top sides were black, with red or blue bottoms, then white bottoms with a deep black top was the fashion until all white with a black top streak became popular. A yawl could be launched quickly, as they were light and could achieve a speed of fifteen miles an hour with a good wind. Stones were used for ballast which could be quite handy as ammunition if you were racing a rival Company!

The Companies took a pride in their yawls, and the names of these vessels became quite well known around the Beach Village. Between 1837 and 1894 the Old Company had four yawls by the name of *Happy New Year*, others being *Princess Royal*, *Southend Friends*, *Beeswing*, *Mosquito*, *Bittern* and *Success*. The Young Company had the *Lord Nelson* and in later days, the *Georgiana*, while the North Roads Company had *Victory* and the *Lady Collyer*.

In the early 1880s nearly three hundred longshoremen belonged to the three Lowestoft Beach Companies, the biggest being the Old Company which had one hundred and nineteen members, while the Young Company had ninety members and the North Roads Company had seventy. By this time, some family names had been on the Company books for three generations! The most frequent names in the Old Company were Burwood and Mewse, with Ayers, Cook, Yallop, Coleman and Smith following closely behind. There were also said to have been three James Ellis's and three William Burwoods! In the Young Company, the most common names were Tyrrell, Capps and Hall while in the North Roads Company Roses and Knights were the most numerous. The Old Company was living up to its name too, and among its members had veterans such as James Yallop, who was recorded as being 88 years of age, Ben Butcher was 85 years, Stephen Butcher 84 years, H. Spurgeon 82 years, John Clark 80 years, Ben Taylor 79 years and Tom Ellis 76 years.

With the demise of sail and the end of fish-carrying, the Beachmen's role was diminishing by the latter half of the nineteenth century. Many trading vessels now had their own pilots aboard and with steam tugs operating from the harbour the yawls had strong competition. The Beachmen had to find other work, and the increasing popularity of the seaside holiday in Victorian times provided an opportunity for taking visitors on pleasure trips along the coast. By the end of the nineteenth century, the large yawls were being kept purely for the prestigious Lowestoft Regatta races. This event was dominated by the Young Company yawls *Eclipse* and later the *Georgiana*, which was presented to them in 1892 by 'The Committee of Gentlemen Admirers of the Beachmen'. In response, the Old Company got their own new yawl, which took the name *Happy New Year*, but had to wait fifteen years and fifteen *Georgiana* victories until it won the very last yawl race in 1907.

Subsequently, the Companies dwindled, and in 1901, the North Roads Company amalgamated with the Young Company. There was another attempt at combining the Old and New Company in 1922, but this lasted just a year. The Young Company eventually closed their books in 1939, the same year that the Old Company launched their last yawl, before closing in 1940. In 1935 one of the last shod concerts was held in the Young Company shod. These concerts were annual events, known as 'smokers', and were peculiar to Lowestoft but by this time had become more of a nostalgic affair, the event recalling the past glories of the Beachmen. The Lowestoft Journal reported on this particular smoker, stating there was ". . . an excellent concert programme . . ." that night. The Company still had sixty members, among them the Coxswain Albert Spurgeon, and it is recorded that the highlight was a duet sang by the brothers Welham, 'Happy' and 'Brassey', which caused much amusement and ". . . refreshments, liquid and otherwise, were provided in abundance, together with plentiful supplies of tobacco, cigarettes and fruit dessert . . ." The concert evenings were always a success and there would be many songs sung into the early hours. The Old Company also held smokers, where 'Posh' Fletcher is said to have often sung a rousing song with the rest of the Company joining in the refrain, which was:

"Don't forget your shipmates,
Don't forget your shipmates,
I 'on't forget my shipmates,
With a whack-fol-the-riddle-lol-the-ri-do!"

Beachmen in their shod. On the far left can be seen Harris Allerton, who lived in East House, the most easterly house in the country. The Allertons were a prominent Beach Village family and Harris was one of thirteen children, two of whom died young. The others were: Herbert, Clifford, Sydney, Gordon and Stanley (twins), Billy, Percy, Clara, Louie and Lottie.

The yawl race at the 1853 Lowestoft Regatta was watched by large crowds on the beach and the North and South Piers. The Eastern Counties Railway ran excursion trains to bring visitors to the town for the regatta, which was an event not only for yachtsmen but also for the Beachmen, whose yawls competed for prize money totalling £30.

The Lowestoft lifeboat Frances Ann setting off to a rescue in the early nineteenth century. This boat was built by Barcham who was situated on the Beach Village near the site where the gasworks would be built.

Two photographic portraits of Beachmen. On the left is Edward 'Ned' Ellis who was coxswain of the volunteer lifeboat, the Caroline Hamilton, in the 1880s. On the right can be seen 'Watcher' Turrell, the well-known Beachman, lifeboatman and great-grandfather of Joy Pearce who contributed to this book.

In addition to the two Company shods, some Beachmen had their own personal hut, where they kept their own fishing gear and bits and pieces. The shod on the left belonged to Harris Allerton who lived at East House which can just be seen behind the other shod which belonged to Jack Rose's father. These shods were situated in Newcombe Road, which was also where Albert Spurgeon's shod was situated, shown below.

Old Fitz and Posh

Perhaps one of the most unlikely stories to come out of the Beach Village was that of the poet and the Beachman, or 'Old Fitz' and 'Posh', as they were known. When the two met, Edward Fitzgerald was a fifty-five year old poet and writer, with a failed marriage and a reputation for eccentricity, living in Market Hill, Woodbridge. He would later become world-renowned for his translation of the Rubaiyat of Omar Khayyam. Joseph 'Posh' Fletcher was his complete opposite, a twenty-five year old Lowestoft Beachman, who lived at 8 Strand Street, earning his living trawling and long-lining supplemented by salvage work with the Old Beach Company.

It was Fitzgerald's fascination with the Beachmen and their stories that formed the basis of this remarkable friendship which began with a chance meeting in 1864 as a result of Joe's father's shrimp boat being stolen. The boat was spotted by coast-guards further down the coast, boarded and moored on the Deben near the Felixstowe Ferry where Joe and his father were to collect her. When they arrived the next day Fitzgerald's yacht happened to lay alongside the shrimper and having heard the news about the boat, 'Old Fitz', as he became known amongst the fishing fraternity, invited them aboard.

Fitzgerald struck up an immediate rapport with the young Posh, who was full of the sea-lore that Fitzgerald found so interesting and would enthusiastically send to his famous friends such as Tennyson and Carlyle. In his schooner named *Scandal*, named after, as he put it, the staple product of Woodbridge, Fitzgerald made regular visits to Lowestoft and always stayed at 12 Marine Terrace in London Road North (now a solicitor's office) in the days when the front of the house was what is now the back, close to the harbour and his new-found friend. However, Fitzgerald knew the town before he met Posh, once writing that he used to wander the town's shore hoping to come across a Beachman whom he could befriend to learn more of their hard life. Later it was found that Posh had noticed his strollings but didn't like to approach Fitz first as he didn't think it becoming.

When in town, Old Fitz and Posh might roam around the North Denes or the harbour or more likely pay a visit to the *Suffolk Hotel*, the old poet's favourite haunt, where he would sit and smoke and listen to the tales of Posh and his friends, their tongues loosened no doubt at Old Fitz's expense. However, they would never go over the bridge to Kirkley as neither fancied mingling with the 'aristocratic gentility,' although the pair did once go to church together at Yarmouth. Fitzgerald also had Fletcher's portrait painted by Samuel Lawrence and even persuaded Posh to pay a visit to a theatre in Lowestoft, for a performance of the Merchant of Venice, during which it is said that the fisherman slumbered peacefully!

Fitz described Posh as 'a man of the finest Saxon type . . . blue eyes, a nose less than Roman, more than Greek, and strictly auburn hair that any woman might sigh to possess . . . a man of simplicity of soul, justice of thought, tenderness of nature, a gentleman of nature's grandest type.' Born at Lowestoft on June 20th 1839, Joseph Delly Fletcher was however very much a Beachman, and like many of his kind was always fond of his drink.

One man who knew Posh Fletcher well was Harris Allerton, a fellow member of the Old Company, who in 1959, at the age of eighty-five, was interviewed by Charles Goodey for an article concerning this friendship which appeared in the East Anglian Daily Times, on 31st March that year. At the time he could even recall having seen Old Fitz and remembered, "He was a big old man who used to go about with a great shawl round his shoulders . . ." Harris however, could well remember Posh, "He was a very nice man was Joe, whatever anybody else may say about him. He was nice old cock – one of the best. He wouldn't harm a cat. He was a man anyone would like provided they were sociable. He was not a bully and was very fond of a joke. He was a fine upright man right to his last days. He was one of our best seamen – a very good fisherman . . ."

In 1867 the friendship of Posh and Old Fitz led to a business partnership when Fitz bought a herring lugger for £360 and Posh contributed the fishing gear as his part of the enterprise. Fitzgerald, ever the poet, named the vessel *Meum and Tuum* (Mine and Thine), which is perhaps derived from the Old Beach saying, "What's thine is mine and what's mine's my own." Unfortunately, although the name painted on the stern was *Meum and Tuum* locally she was called Mum Tum! Registered on 3 August 1867, this vessel was 47' 4" long with 15' beam and 6' 7" depth of hold. She had a black hull with yellow beadings and her name on the transom was picked out in gold letters on a scarlet background.

Despite the catches showing a profit of £450 at the end of the first year, Fletcher was never a businessman and all the money was spent clearing debts which he had allowed to mount up. Things didn't improve and eventually the partnership broke up and the Mum Tum was sold and continued to fish the North Sea until she became unseaworthy. She was broken up in 1888 and her nameboard purchased and donated to the Omar Khayyam Club. Posh took over another boat, the *Henrietta* with Fitzgerald as mortgagee but soon after New Year's Day 1869, Fitz was back at Lowestoft writing, "I came here two days ago to wind up the lugger's account." This too was sold with Old Fitz receiving the proceeds.

One of the main problems of this partnership was revealed by Albert Spurgeon, one time coxswain of Lowestoft lifeboat, who was also interviewed by Goodey for his research. Spurgeon was a longshoreman who spent his whole life on the Beach and as a lad knew Posh, "I used to be his lapdog as a boy. He used to lay his boat alongside ours and I used to see after it for him, especially when he used to get his 'dowry' as he called it from Old Fitz. He used to go on the booze when it arrived and I wouldn't see anything much of him until the money had gone."

Harris Allerton though, who could also remember seeing the Mum Tum boat in and around the port, did not agree that alchohol was the only problem, "I wouldn't say drink was his downfall. Of course, he liked his pint but I think his worst trouble was his wife. She was one of those hell-cat women and was forever scrubbing her linen props and those sort of things and that was what made him get an extra pint aboard at times."

Mason Ayers was Fletcher's last surviving relative, a veteran fish market merchant and also a trustee of the Fishermen's Bethel. Ayers was living on the Beach when he gave Charles Goodey his verdict on his uncle, which perhaps shows another side of Fletcher's decline, "He was a fine-looking chap in his early days, that's probably why he got the nickname Posh. When he first became a skipper he was a very good fisherman but all that changed after Old Fitz bought him the Mum Tum. He was properly spoiled by the old man who used to take him to some of his posh dinners and made rather a fool of him. They used to go a lot to the old *Suffolk Hotel* where Fitz used to treat him to drinks and he got so that he did not go to sea when he ought to have done. Drink was his worst enemy and Old Fitz properly ruined him, there's no doubt about that . . . You couldn't call him (Posh) a likeable man. My father didn't think much of him, not when he gave way to drink and he left my aunt

(Above):

*4–11 Strand Street. In the 1870s Joseph 'Posh'
Fletcher lived at No. 8, which is by the woman
and baby. The western part of Strand Street
contained two more houses and No. 2 was
where Robert Sterry lived.*

(Right):

*A portrait of Joseph
'Posh' Fletcher, in his
thirties, circa 1870.*

Edward Fitzgerald
1809–1883

in a bad way. They had five or six children but most of them died of consumption. His downfall was drink and, in many ways, that was due to Fitzgerald . . ."

After the failure of the business, Fitzgerald and Fletcher drifted apart, although Old Fitz did keep in touch for a while with letters, and the old poet, about to go to Lowestoft in 1877, could still write kindly of his friend. "The Great Man . . . is yet there: commanding a Crew of those who prefer being his Men to having a command of his own . . . His Glory is somewhat marred: but he looks every inch a King in his lugger now. At home (when he is there and not at the Tavern) he sits among his Dogs, Cats, Birds, etc. always with a great Dog following all round and abroad. This is the Greatest Man I have known . . ." In 1893 Fitzgerald died and was buried in Boulge churchyard.

After the break-up of the partnership Posh fished on other luggers but in the end was reduced to scraping a living from shrimping and whatever else he could pick up. After his wife died in 1892, Posh lodged for the next fourteen years with Mrs Capps at 2 Chapel Street and was often to be found in one of two beer houses in the north of the town.

Life was not kind to him in his last years, as Albert Spurgeon described, "He lived at one time in Duke's Head Street, but later lived in an old bathing machine on a bit of land near my home in Newcombe Road. He took off the wheels and laid it on four stones off the beach and when the Corporation people tried to shift him, he claimed squatter's rights and they couldn't move him." Indeed, the last time Mason Ayers saw his Uncle Joe was when he was cooking herring "over Beamish the blacksmith's fire down on the Beach."

By this time the letters from Fitzgerald that Posh had amassed were worth a small fortune as the poet's reputation had grown since his death, or they would have been had he kept them intact and handled them wisely. Seemingly unaware of their potential value, Posh had frittered them away over the years, telling author James Blyth, who was writing a book about Fitzgerald and Fletcher, that he had "torn up sackfuls of 'em and strewn them to the winds." Others had been given away for a pittance with Fletcher complaining to Blyth about one man who called to see him. "He axed me about the guv'nor," explained Posh, "and for me to show him any letters I had. He took a score or so away w'im and I told him a sight of things, thinking he was a gentleman . . . he gave me one drink of whisky and that's all I see of him. He was off with the letters and all and never gave me a farden . . . I heerd arterwards as the letters was sold by auction for thutty pounds . . ."

Harris Allerton had also come across some of these precious letters and told the story to Charles Goodey, "He finished up in a shed only big enough for one man to sit in, not far from my house," said Harris, "and I used to go and have a talk with him. He had sold his bigger shed to Burrows the boat-owner when he was hard up and I saw Burrows clearing it out. There wasn't much in it and I asked Joe if he still had any letters from Old Fitz. He said he couldn't remember but as I sat outside mending my nets one day I saw Burrows come out of the shed with a kipper box and a shovel. He dug a hole and emptied the box in and, being curious, I went back later and unburied the stuff. I found forty or fifty letters Old Fitz had written to Joe and I knew they must be worth plenty of good money. I read some of them – I remember Old Fitz asked in one about a new stove he had fitted in Joe's cottage. I could have kept the letters myself – it wouldn't have been stealing, would it? But I thought, 'Poor old Joe, he's hard up. They won't do me any good.' He used to bring me bits of stuff out of his shed and sell them to me and when he came next morning I gave him the letters."

"I told him: 'You know they are worth money, don't make a fool of them.' I knew where he would take them. He thanked me and went to Fred Ecclestone's pub up in Crown Street and sold them to somebody for £20. Three days after that, I went back to the hole to see if I could find any more and dug up another four or five that had been spoiled through being left in the ground. Still, they were readable and I kept them until a few years ago when I happened to catch my sister just about to burn them on the kitchen fire. I rescued them and sold them for £1 to Mr Mallett who used to write in the papers about us old Beachmen."

Life continued to be a struggle for Posh, and at one time when he was ill, he was taken to Oulton Workhouse but came back to his little hut again. In 1909 he obtained an old age pension but on September 17th, 1915, at the age of seventy-six, Posh died a pauper in Oulton Workhouse from heart failure due to senile decay and chronic bronchitis.

Whether he was a drunken rogue or an unfortunate hero, he was definitely the most well-known of the Lowestoft fishermen of his era though perhaps unable to handle his brush with fame. He was remembered fondly by many locals though," He was real old Beachman," said Albert Spurgeon, "not a scrounger like some of them but a real good old sort."

"He was a fine upright man," said Harris Allerton. "You couldn't call him likeable," said his nephew, Mason Ayers. There may have been a difference of opinion about the man Joseph 'Posh' Fletcher, pictured here towards the end of his life, but there is no doubt that he was a colourful character and a typical Beachman.

Despite the demise of the Beach Companies, the presence of Beachmen in the lifeboat crews continued. Throughout the history of the lifeboat in Lowestoft, most of the coxswains have lived in the Beach Village. Robert Hook is a fine example of a Beachman and lifeboatman. He was coxswain of the lifeboat from 1853 to 1883, and a member of the Old Company too. By the age of sixteen Bob was six foot three tall with an Herculian frame and he was already helping to save lives at sea. By the time of his retirement he had twice won the Institution's Silver Medal. Hook retired in 1883, owing to a dispute with the Lifeboat Institution over paying his crew in his pub called the *Fishermen's Arms*, opposite the *Rising Sun*, in premises that would later be Hammond's fish and chip shop. Hook came from a Beach Village family, and had a brother who was known as 'Sheppey', supposedly because he wore his tan 'slop' so long that he looked like a shepherd. In the Lowestoft Journal on September 11th 1886 Robert Hook explained a little of his famous history, "I was born on 4th June 1828 and am therefore just over 58 years old. My father was Robert Hook, a fisherman and Beachman who died a few years ago aged 86 years. My grandfather was 87 years old when he died in 1844 and both had been long connected with lifeboat service in one way or another." Robert Hook died on 28th June 1911 aged 83, and was survived by his wife, Sarah Ann Hook, who died seven years later on 18th January 1918.

Another notable coxswain of the lifeboat was John 'Jack' Swan who was born in 1857. He was also a member of the Old Company, coming from a large Beach family which it is said at one time had three generations in the Company. From an early

On the left is Robert Hook, who was conxswain of the Lowestoft lifeboat for thirty years and a member of the Old Company, along with his brother William 'Sheppey' Hook, pictured right

age Jack was involved with yawls and he was a member of the lifeboat crew for fifty-two years and in 1911, at the age of fifty-four, he was appointed coxswain of the Lowestoft lifeboat.

One of the most spectacular rescues with which he was involved was when the lifeboat *Agnes Cross* put to sea in a fierce gale in response to a distress call from the *Hopelyn*. The vessel had run aground on Scroby Sands and had been battered by huge seas. Despite jagged parts of the wreck sticking up all round, Swan managed to steer his lifeboat right up close and save twenty-four lives and even the ship's cat! Swan was awarded the R.N.L.I. Gold Medal for this service and the house where he lived, which was next to the Alms Houses on Whapload Road, became known as Hopelyn Cottage as a result of this rescue.

In June 1924 Swan retired after helping to save 258 lives in Institution boats with over seventy launches as coxswain. He had been awarded two Silver Medals in addition to the Gold and he was further honoured by King George V with an O.B.E. on 30th June 1924 at Buckingham Palace. During his retirement Jack became an elder statesman for the R.N.L.I. and spent his time supporting the service by presenting prizes, or speaking at theatres and cinemas in London and was even heard on the radio. He died on 2nd February 1935 at the age of seventy-eight but three of his sons followed him into the lifeboat service.

Jack Swan was fondly remembered in the Beach Village and is still well thought of today. Ronny James remembers him as an old man, "He was a fine old fellow with a white beard. I was in Lowestoft Hospital with him. I lay in the next bed to him and as he'd won several awards he had a lot of influential friends who used to bring him fruit which was a luxury in those days. When they'd gone he'd say, 'Come on boy, you have these!' He was a nice old chap he was. He used to say, 'Take 'em all round the ward!'"

Swan's successor as coxswain was Albert Spurgeon. As a crew member of the *Agnes Cross* he received the Bronze Medal in November 1922 for his part in the *Hopelyn* rescue and in 1924 he took over the command. In November 1927 he was awarded the Silver Medal for his rescue of the crew of the ketch *Lily of Devon*. He became coxswain of the *Michael Stephens* in 1939, and in November 1943 he was awarded the Bronze 2nd Service Clasp for his rescue of the crew of *H.M. Minesweeper No. 106*. He retired in 1947 after twenty-three years as coxswain. Charles Ellis recalls that Albert Spurgeon was the proud possessor of a a pair of binoculars, given to him by a German captain during the First World War. "He reckoned that the L52 Zeppelin came down off Lowestoft and the lifeboat picked up the survivors. Spurgeon pulled the captain into the lifeboat and he had a set of night-glasses round his neck. He said, 'Thank you very much,' and taking the glasses from his neck he hung them round old Spurgeon's neck and said in first-class English, 'You might as well have these, I shan't need them any more in this war.' And Spurgeon always had those glasses."

The link between the Beach Village and the lifeboat continued into the 1960s and beyond. Harry Burgess lived on the Grit, and was a lifeboat crew member from 1931 to 1936 and bowman from 1937 to 1946. In 1947 he was made second coxswain and in the same year was appointed coxswain at which time he was the youngest coxswain on the East Coast. More recent coxswains have been Peter Gibbons and John Catchpole who both have connections with the Beach.

Vernil Tuck was typical of this breed of Beachmen and lifeboatmen. Said to have been the last surviving member of the Old Company, Vernil lived with his wife and

John Swan (above) was coxswain from 1911 to 1924 when he retired at the age of seventy-two. He won the Institution's Gold Medal, the Silver Medal twice, and was also awarded the O.B.E. His successor was Albert Spurgeon (left), who was coxswain from 1924 until his retirement in 1947. Albert won the Institution's Silver Medal and twice won the bronze.

his three daughters at 27 Wilde's Street, but later, in the early 1960s when this property was being demolished, he moved with his wife to Lighthouse Score until his death on August 3rd 1987. One of his daughters, Beryl Clover, recalls her father talking about his early days in the lifeboat. She remembers, "Because his name was Tuck, they used to call him 'Friar' Tuck. He was in the lifeboat from a very early age. He used to go there to sweep up at first, because he wanted to get in the lifeboat." Norma takes up the story, ". . . Because he was young they used to make him sweep up and clean the wood and put it in the burner. He went there when he was fifteen and we don't think he was credited with all the years he was there. Because he was known as 'Friar', some of his early years were credited to Friar instead. Later he was known as just 'Tucky'." His first name, Vernil, was unique to the Beach Village in a way. Beryl explains, "When he was born in 1907, he should have been Vernon, but they spelt it wrong at the christening, or at least, that's what he always said!"

"I can remember when my father used to go out on the lifeboat," adds Norma. "When the rockets went up we all had our own little jobs, one had to get his boots out ready for him, while the other was getting his bike out of the shed. My Mum used to get his coat, Sheila used to get his tobacco and that, we all knew our jobs, then he used to get on his bike, and we all used to race down beside him. There was a slipway by the lifeboat shed and we raced down with my Dad and all the children in the road used to go as well, and we'd all stand on the sea wall, and the lifeboat-men would wave on their way out. We used to wait for them to come in and sometimes our hands were all frost bitten."

Yvonne Scriggins' father John Scriggins, who was also known as Jack or 'Pimp', died in January 1996. At one time he was a was a lifeboatman on the *Agnes Cross*. "When on lifeboat duty Dad was knocked up to go to a rescue, more often than not he would have to put on wet trousers which had been drying in front of the fire. They were his only pair."

Ron James' father was also a lifeboatman. "I've known a time when my father would go to the pub and have a couple of pints, come home and be just going to bed and the lifeboat guns would go, and he'd run like hell down there and that was supposed to be his day off, and he'd be out in the lifeboat! They used to run right along to the North Pier, we used to call it the Old Extension, they used to have to run all the way and I don't know how many, but people have died just running there, collapse with a heart attack I suppose, we didn't know much about that then, they were dead and we just buried them!"

After the Second World War the compensation received for damage to the Beach Company sheds was used to fund The Lifeboat and Life Saving Apparatus Club and their headquarters were erected near the coastguard station on the north beach.

Most of the lifeboat crew in the 1960s had connections with the Beach Village. Here the crew are pictured on the boarding boat with the lifeboat Frederick Edward Crick in the background. (From the top, clockwise) Billy Capps Jenner, Billy Thorpe, Harold Robinson, Jack Rose, Harry Kirby, Harry Burgess (coxswain), Peter Gibbons, Jock Stoddart, Vernil Tuck.

Thomas 'Brock' Ellis, weighed 24 stone and was the biggest man in the port in his day. It seems likely this is the Brock Ellis who in 1835 was one of the crew of a beach yawl which capsized off Yarmouth after putting men on board a Spanish brig, the Paquette de Bilboa, to help pump her out and pilot her into the harbour. However, the ship went down and after swimming for seven and a half hours through an October night, covering fifteen miles before being picked up by the brig Betsy of Sunderland, Brock was in poor shape, his throat was highly inflamed and swollen, his neck, chest, hands and feet completely flayed but he was the only survivor.

4

Gritsters

*"... It is fairly true to say that every person
on the Beach was a character in their own right ..."*

LEONARD ADAMS

"The Lowestoft beach population are in every sense of the term a peculiar people," said an article in the Lowestoft Journal, in the early 1900s, "from the earliest childhood inured to hardship and contention with the cruel sea, which they regard as the natural enemy, the merciless devourer of their kindred, and many widows and orphans. They acquire a sturdy independence of character unknown to the citizens of inland towns. They have inter-married for generations amongst their own particular class, and there are few Beach families, we believe, which are not like the Highland clans. They are generally speaking a quiet unobtrusive class of persons, but when the latent 'Viking' spirit is aroused in their breasts, they are like the ocean in a storm."

This independence on the Beach was sometimes taken to such a degree that people from the town would not mix with those who lived below the cliff. There was a feeling that the town folk literally looked down on people from the Beach which served only to isolate this small fishing community and fire up the spirit amongst them. Alan Doy recalls a story which illustrates this isolation from the rest of the town. "My grandparents' name was Cullum, and they lived at 3 Rant Score East and had several children, one of whom was my mother, Agnes. Boys from the town wouldn't take out Beach girls and if they did there would be a bit of a fuss. When my mother started dating my father she didn't want him to know where she lived so when he used to take her home, she would say goodbye to him at her friend's house in the High Street. Then she used to go through to the back of the house and slide on her bottom down the cliff and go home that way!"

"My father's father was quite wealthy and when he found out that his son was going out with a Beach girl he didn't like it. He threatened to cut him off from the family so my father told him to stick his money. When my parents married they lived in Kimberley Road in the town and my mother's sister went to live in Tonning Street, but as soon as their husbands had gone to work the girls went back to the Beach; that's where they belonged ..."

Beach people were known by a variety of names, such as 'Pea Bellies', 'Sand Chompers' or 'Gritsters' and they certainly proved themselves to be a unique breed, showing great strength of character in times of adversity. Generations of families lived on the Beach, and some surnames had long association with the place, such as Mewse, Capps, Rose, Ayers, Liffen, Cook, Burwood, Swan, Hook, Norman and Dalley.

One of the most popular and memorable characters in living memory seems to be Alfred 'Happy' Welham. Happy died in the late 1930s having lived in the Fishermen's Cottages at 16 Lighthouse Score for most of his life – for thirty-seven years by 1900. Lenny 'Winky' Norman remembers, "Now Happy never did wash, only if it rained! He used to have a chimney sweep business but in the fishing time my Dad used to say that he'd go along and cart all the gear for them at a tanner a time or whatever they could afford. He'd cart the oilies and boots and that back to the houses, his dog with him . . . when the cart was full, his little old dog would run along underneath. I've seen old Happy that drunk that the little old dog would have the reins of the donkey in his mouth and drive all the way along Whapload Road till they got home. The dog would take old Happy home!"

In addition to carrying the fishermen's clothes to the docks in his cart for a few shillings, during the First World War Happy also did this for the Navy. It was around this time that he retired his faithful old donkey and bought a little black and white pony but his donkey obviously meant a lot to him as it is said that during one of the many floods of the Beach Village he took the animal upstairs into a bedroom for safety! Happy also had a little terrier dog, called Spot, who always used to travel around with him, sitting alongside him in the pony trap.

One particular story concerning Happy occurred in 1916 when the German Navy bombarded the town. An unexploded shell fell into Lighthouse Score and Happy, never one to miss an opportunity, is supposed to have grabbed a broom and rolled the shell into his garden, charging passers-by tuppence to see the new 'exhibit'! However, not everyone agrees with this version of events. Benny Knights explains, "This yarn about Happy Welham rolling it into his garden and charging tuppence, well, he couldn't move that in his garden! I'll tell you what happened to that. I was seven years old at the time and I was running along Whapload Road on that day and as the guns went off I jumped in the air. When the shell hit the wall and fell onto the road, it faced Happy's garden wall, so he came out with a broom and swivelled it round so that it faced the Denes in case it went off! The Navy came about three days later with a lorry and took it away!"

During the summer months Happy would put a notice above his front door saying, 'If you are dry, Come in and try, Happy's Home Made Drink.' This was a wine that he and his wife, whom the local children used to call Aunt Phoebe, made in their kitchen along with lemonade for which they charged a halfpenny a bottle.

Happy died shortly before his cottage was due to be demolished in the late 1930s. Ronny Woolner recalls, "It was one Christmas. We realized that nobody had seen Happy or his wife for two or three days. I lived in the 'Shoals', just at the bottom of Lighthouse Score, and nobody had seen them. So my father and another man fetched a ladder and got through their window. They were both lying there ill. They took Happy away and he died but his wife was okay and she moved away and lived until after the Second World War."

Bill Cooper lived at 38 Whapload Road, and remembers, "There were two chimney sweeps on the Beach. There was Happy Welham of course, and Jakie Smith. There were a lot of characters on the Beach. There was a character called Rackham. He used to walk about with a basket of smoked fish on his head, selling them. Then there was the Old Pot Buyer. This was a bloke who used to push this handcart full of old chamber pots. Plain ones tuppence each, the ones with flowers on threepence"

'Happy' Welham pictured with his pony and his little terrier dog, called Spot. "... I've seen old Happy that drunk," says Lenny Norman, "that the little dog would have the reins of the donkey in his mouth and take that all the way along Whapload Road till they got home! ..."

'Happy' lived at 16 Lighthouse Score, which was the end cottage nearest to Whapload Road, for over seventy years.

Another memorable character was Daisy Dinks, who seems to have been quite a girl in her day. Daisy lived on the Beach for many years, right up until its demise. Jean Mitchell remembers, "The last year we lived on the Beach, 1965, I worked in Squire's shop on the corner of Whapload Road and Wilde's Street. Mr Squire was just winding down the business and his best customer in that last year was 'Old Daisy' as she was known. She was particularly known by our American Allies during the war and often gave Mum a tin of spam or corned beef for our dinner. Although my Mum didn't approve of her way of life, she never refused these tins, as they were a luxury during the war."

Godfrey Girling was a barber in the Beach Village in the 1930s and saw many characters in his line of work, such as 'Dickie-Bird' Rose, a distant relation of Jack Rose, who lived next door to one of Jack's uncles in the Alms Houses in Whapload Road. "I knew old Dickie-Bird," laughs Godfrey. "He used to come in mine. I used to say, 'Hello, Dickie,' I thought that was his name, but it wasn't. Some bloke said to me, you shouldn't call him that! He got had up once for saying to the kids, do you want to come and see my little dickie-bird!"

Godfrey also remembers Joe Catchpole. "He came in mine one morning, poor old fella, he was a little bit slow, but a good old boy really. I said to him, 'How are you getting on, Joe?' and he said to me, 'I want you to do me a kindness, I want you to cut my throat!' So I said, 'If that's what you want, I'll oblige you!' and he kept running on about having his throat cut. So I got him in the chair and lathered him up, and I got this old cut throat razor, dipped it in boiling water, shut the razor up, and said , 'Are you sure you want me to do it, Joe?' He said, 'Yeah, go on,' so I said, 'Right,' and drew the closed razor across his throat, and that was hot. He grabbed his throat and jumped out of the chair, yelling like hell. I was just as mad as they were!"

"Another great character down there," recalls Lenny Norman, "was Nathan 'Slasher' Pickess. He was as big and broad as anyone could be, strong as an ox but he liked his beer. He was that strong he could pick a barrel up and sling it in the air. He was a well known character. His son Freddie was another notable character; if he didn't like you, he'd hit you!" The Norman family themselves were Beach folk, Lenny's parents running the *Suffolk Fishery Tavern* in the 1920s. Lenny's father Robert and brother Bob, both took the nickname 'Umshi' and although the family left the Beach Village, they always had links with the place and Bob returned in the 1950s and took a house alongside the *Gas House Tavern* where he lived until it was demolished in the 1960s.

Ron James can remember another man who had connections with a public house on the Beach. Billy Jones was his name, and his parents ran the *Princess Royal*, situated in Nelson Road. Ron recalls, "Billy Jones' mother used to keep the *Princess Royal* but Billy was a lorry driver for Arthur and Sam Boardley and I believe he was the first man ever to drive a lorry from here to Aberdeen with a load of fish nets. You see, when they were fishing, they used to do so many weeks up there but during that time the nets had to be repaired or tanned, as they called it, to preserve the nets. So Billy had to take a whole fleet of nets up and bring them back and he was the first bloke ever to do it. And you think of those little roads in them days, from here to Aberdeen was a heck of a long way."

"Then there was old Billy Day," Ron continues. "There was a firm down there called Gooderham, he was a coal merchant. Now there was a little fella who worked for them, he was very little. I suppose he was well under five foot and poor old boy he was a lovely lad, but the coal merchant used to have the horse and he never got off the cart to deliver it but he used to say, 'Billy, hundredweight up here, hundredweight there, run, you bugger, run!' And he used to have a sack of coal on his back and he used to run everywhere. The merchant couldn't get his horse and cart up Spurgeon Score so he used to stay at the bottom and poor old Billy used to run all the way up and back with a hundredweight of coal and he'd be running like this all day. He was a real hard grafter . . . They used to slit one corner of the sack and wear it like a hood and then sling a sack of coal over their shoulder, but that empty sack was heavy, without the coal as well!"

"'Darkie' George was another one. He was a binman who used to get as drunk as a lord at the *Rising Sun* or somewhere like that every other Saturday and they used to go and get his missus and put him in a wheelbarrow and push him home. There were no drinking and driving problems in those days!"

"There were a lot of characters down there," Ronny Wilson recalls. "Like Deafy, he used to come along the Beach with a golf ball, and knock the golf ball right from where the fish market is, right the way up to the golf course, he was deaf and dumb. Then there was an old tramp, called 'Puggy' Utting. At one time he lived in the opening where Boardley's carts used to be."

Mr E. J. Day remembers, "There was the rat catcher, old Bob Stigles. He lived by the church, and another well known man was the one-armed barrel organ man who used to play outside pubs and he used to let us play the organ while he went round with his hat."

There were many nicknames on the Beach, and although in some cases the origins of these names have been forgotten, there are a few where the stories behind the names have been passed down. One of the oddest nicknames was Tom 'Tar-the-Clock' Liffen. It seems that on one occasion Tim was painting the front room and painted over the clock too! Michael Duncan didn't discover the origins of his father's nickname 'Tishy' till after he died. "My Uncle Dick and my father, both fishermen, joined Harry Tate's Navy as my father told me, for the duration of the war and both returned to a life-time of fishing afterwards. My father's friends were all from the fishing fraternity and his name was Charlie but most of these people called him 'Tishy'. It never occurred to me to ask him why and I didn't find out until after his death at the gathering of family and friends on the day of my father's cremation. I asked my Uncle Dick why they called my father 'Tishy'. He said that when they were young boys, they used to play along the Denes with their mates and on one occasion they were playing along the top of the area above the Denes Oval and had a race from top to bottom. My father came last and apparently a few days before that a horse named 'Tishy' came last in a big race, I think he said the Grand National, so they nick-named him after that."

Charles Ellis recalls many characters who lived on the Beach. Charles lived in Scarle's Buildings and one of his neighbours was a typical Beach character by the name of Mrs Palmer. "Mrs Palmer had been our next-door neighbour for years and she was quite a character who had many run-ins with old Scarle, our landlord. I think he was a solicitor by trade, lived in Norwich, and you've seen those Victorian cartoons of the old rent men? Well, he was just like that. He had a big, bulbous, red nose, and he always had a Gladstone bag which he put the money in. Times were hard and Mrs Palmer had a family to keep and her old man, Billy Palmer, had one eye. He used to wear a bowler hat and a patch over his eye. He was just a hanger-on down the fish market, he'd pick up a bob here and a bob there. I mean he never had a real job so they were bloody hard up. Scarle came after the rent one day, when they owed several weeks rent and said, 'I've come for the rent Mrs Palmer,' and she say, 'You'll get your rent when I get some money, my family comes first.' He said, 'Mrs Scarle and I were never blessed with children.' 'Your old woman,' she say, 'she ought to have married a fisherman, she'd have plenty of kids then!' "

"I know for a fact that she owed £46 for bread, and in those days that was a lot of money. Her boy Percy went into one of the top boats, the ones that always earned the money, and he did well once and she paid off every penny. She wouldn't avoid paying. Old Scarle went round there once near Christmas. And he say to her, 'What are you going to have for Christmas dinner?' She say, 'Well, it's like this Mr Scarle. If the boats do well we're going to have a turkey and a Christmas pudding. If they don't do very well we'll have a red herring and close the curtains!' "

Charles remembers that when Mrs Palmer died, a rumour began to spread around the Beach that her house was haunted. He continues, "Mrs Palmer had been a big woman who always used to wear a white apron, spotlessly white, and some people said they saw her standing in the doorway with this white apron on. In the house doors would open, they'd hear footsteps, that sort of thing. I used to think it was a guilty conscience, you know, they felt guilty they hadn't done enough for her when she was alive. After school, the kids used to go round to Scarle's Buildings to see if they could see her ghost. One night my father wanted some tobacco, so he say to me, 'Here you are boy, go and get me some cigarette paper,' but it was dark so I stood in the doorway and I wasn't very keen on going. So he say, 'What the hell is up with you?' So I say, 'I might see Mrs Palmer.' He say, 'Come you here. You knew Mrs Palmer when she was alive. She used to give you sweets, didn't she? Did she ever do you any harm?' I shook my head. 'Well then,' he said, 'if she didn't do you any bloody harm when she was alive she isn't going to do any when she's dead. Go get me my tobacco!' I always remember that, because after that I never was scared."

"The keys for the front doors in Scarle's Buildings would fit the other houses in the row, and our key fitted Mrs Palmer's door. One night about ten o'clock, just before my old man was getting ready to go to bed, there was a knock on the door, and there were three or four of these clients that reckon they can see ghosts. They had packs on their backs with all that paraphernalia. My Dad said, 'What do you want Mister, this time of night?' So one of them say, 'Well, we hear there is a ghost two doors away, where Mrs Palmer used to live, and we want to see for ourselves.' You see, with the house being empty, they wanted to sleep there the night, and one of them said to my old man, 'We understand that your key will fit the door,' but he wasn't having none of it. He say, 'You get off my doorstep, you'll not get my key, and if you get in that bloody house, I'll come and kick you out. If Mrs Palmer's ghost is there, you leave her alone. She lived there all them years and if she want to stop there that's her business, not yours.' This bloke and his mates, they scuttled out of the yard, they were gone out of sight right quick. My old man soon put a stop to them."

During the depression of the 1930s, Charles worked in Ayers' fish house as a way of getting some money. It was here that he encountered more fiery characters who lived on the Grit and remembers one in particular. "They were hard down there all right, but they had to live that way because that was how it was. Old Maud Wilson worked with me at Ayers', she was a West Indian and weighed about sixteen stone. She was a nice woman really but she didn't stand any nonsense. She was one of the women cutting the herring for kippers, and these women were each allotted a girl who was paid about half as much to pack the fish. Well, the women used to be there sometimes before six in the morning so they could get their day's work done. Betty, she was a cheeky little beggar, was allocated to Maud, and she was never on time. She couldn't get up I suppose, and it was a hell of a time to get up in the morning. So Betty was always late and it put Maud late and she got fed up with it. So eventually she say, 'Betty, if you're late tomorrow morning, I'll show you what we used to do to the girls at Sayer and Holloway's.' Well, the next morning Betty was late again. When she turned up Maud say, 'You're late again girl!' and she say, 'Yes, Maud,' and before Betty could say anything else, Maud grabbed hold of her, and lifted her with one hand, straight across the bench face down. She was up with this girl's skirt, pulled the knickers down, so there was her bare behind. There were these plates that were used with a stiff brush and black lead to stamp the fish boxes. Maud slapped one on her behind and put 'Best Bloaters' across her, and then she pulled up her knickers and said, 'Now be late tomorrow' . . ."

✳   ✳   ✳   ✳

A Beach reunion at Jack's retirement party in 1991. (Left to right) Billy Keith, Jack Reynolds, Jack Rose and Gus Jensen.

John Rose, who lived in Vigilant Cottages and later in the Alms Houses, was a Beachman and lifeboatman. Here he is shown talking to a young Harry Burgess who later became the coxswain on the lifeboat.

5

Childhood

"In the Beach Village there was plenty for children to do,
but you made it yourself. There was no rowdiness like today . . ."

BILLY KEITH

Growing up on the Beach, in the early part of the twentieth century was very different from children's lives today. With the whole of the Denes to play on, the north beach nearby and freedom to roam the streets, many of the people who grew up at this time speak of their happiness in spite of the hardship of the time. Although they may not have had the computers and toys of the present younger generation, the Beach boys and girls made their own fun. However even in the 1920s and '30s, children's games were subject to fashion. Ruby Timberley remembers, "There always seemed to be seasons when certain toys were the 'in' thing. When the shops started selling wooden tops and whips every child wanted a top and a lot of fun was had in seeing who could whip their top and make it spin the longest. Then the time came for wooden hoops with a stick to bowl them along Whapload Road. No problem with traffic in those days, we could see and hear the odd horse and cart coming, and we just let it pass and carried on bowling or whipping. Sometimes if the weather was hot, the tar melted on the road and stuck to your shoes, or feet if you had no shoes on. Then marbles were 'in' and no end of fun was had. We children had bags to keep them in . . . there were different kinds of marbles, the glass ones were called alleys."

"As the weather got colder, skipping for girls was the thing. Single skipping ropes with wooden handles, costing one penny, were a girl's pride and joy, and mothers' clothes lines were very handy when a number of girls wanted to skip on the pickling plots (before the Scots girls came). Two girls would each hold one end of the rope and turn it, calling to their comrades to run and jump in and skip, usually to a rhyme or a number, then change over so every one had a turn."

Mrs Jessie Hitter (née Harper) was from an earlier generation, born in 1903, but she also used to play marbles, "Me and Esther Garrod used to play on Christ Church Square, we used to make a hole to play marbles, but she always used to win. We also used to play skipping ropes and wooden tops." During the summer the children would spend hours on the beach. Mrs Hitter continues, "The boys used to run down the beach with no bathing costumes on, while the girls used to have to go in the sea with flannelette drawers on, we never had bathing costumes . . . we used to run down the beach with no shoes on. In the summertime the boys never had shoes or socks on, couldn't afford them."

51

Ethel Baker (née Thompson) remembers, "I used to play around the boat sheds or on the pickling plots. We were given a bottle of water and bread and lard sandwiches and told to stay out all day."

"We spent hours on the beach," recalls Mrs Timberley," running or walking bare-foot from home to the beach, we made sandcastles, designs made of pebbles in sand – we leap-frogged, jumped off the sea wall, and ran in and out of the sea, and lots more. In the afternoons the mothers came with the babies, and to gossip with each other. This all sounds very nice and I think we were very fortunate to live so near the sea, although when the sea was rough in the winter we could hear the roaring and splashing of the waves indoors. Sometimes we saw a horse being brought down to the sea in hot weather to walk through the sea to cool its feet with the man still sitting on the horse."

Born in 1928, Mr Eric Horne also has fond memories of those far-off days of sunshine. He remembers, "In the summer holidays, whole days would be spent playing on the beach, with a packed lunch and tea taken along, consisting of sand-wiches and a bottle of home-made lemonade . . . My eldest brother sometimes had a Sunday swim in the sea off what we called the Second Denes. I would sit on the beach beside his towel and clothes, and afterwards he would give me a piggy-back all the way to a shop near the bottom of Wilde's Score and treat me to a halfpenny ice-cream cornet, served from a two-compartment wooden affair on wheels, which stood outside the shop. There was a difficult choice to be made between vanilla and strawberry."

Ronny Wilson was born on the Beach, and lived at 4 East Street, opposite the *Rising Sun*, his mother running a sweet shop at the bottom of Spurgeon Score. ". . . We lived in East Street. My mother took up a business at the bottom of Spurgeon Score, a sweet business in a shop that used to be Cook's the butchers. My father was a fisherman, a chief engineer, so we were a little bit richer than the others, so I was the one who paid tuppence to go in the *Regent*, and go down the back to the toilet and open the window to let all the others in. About twenty of us in for tuppence!"

Ronny fondly remembers the Denes swimming pool, ". . . and outside of that you had a children's playground with swings and roundabouts and the boating lake. We used to go swimming from the beach though, in fact, when I was a boy we used to sleep on the beach. We slept down there right through the summer period, we spent four weeks down there and never went home, except to wash our clothes out. My mother used to give us a few spuds and a bit of lard, and we slept down there in an old sack tent, behind the gasworks. We used to go down on the market, knock off a couple of herring, light a fire, split them, put them on the fire and roast them for our dinner. There was me, I was called 'Titch' Wilson, 'Hockey' Pickess, Troy Harper, there was Harry Harper, Claude Dalley, and the Prettymans."

This gang included Bert Prettyman. "That's where we used to be all the sum-mer," remembers Bert, "in our tent on the beach, the whole lot of us. Our mothers knew where to find us."

Benny Knights, although older, also spent the summers of his youth camping out in this area, "The foreman at Gourock Ropeworks used to give us boys a bell tent which we used to pitch on the Denes and in the summertime we used to live down there, every night. We used to get potatoes and stew up, we had a hell of a time."

The shingle mill on the North Extension also provided an impromptu 'swimming pool' for the boys. Billy Keith lived in Cook's Buildings in the south of the Beach

Village, and recalls, "The cranes dug out a huge area, somewhere like ten to fifteen feet or deeper, and the tide would come in and fill it up. We used to stand on the quay and dive in, we had our own swimming pool!"

Ronny Wilson also remembers these 'dykes' as they were known locally. "While we were there 'Penny' the copper used to be waiting at the other end for us to come off, so we had to climb on the sand wagon, bury ourselves in sand and breathe through a straw till we got past the corner, and we used to jump off near the bridge and go home. 'Course, he used to wait for us. He was all right though, Penny was, he was a good policeman. He used to give you a crack over the head or a boot up the backside, but if you told your father, you'd get another one, so you used to keep quiet about it."

"There were some rafts down there too," Ronny continues, "that were used for painting the boats. They used to leave them in the harbour, tied up, and we used to get them and go out on them. One day we were on one of them, there were three lots of rafts, and we were stuck in the middle. So old Penny, he come along and say, 'Right! I want you lot!' So I say to the others, you go that way and we'll go the other and get ashore, and when he comes chasing after us, you can get ashore, but he never even bothered! He just wheeled our bicycles up the police station and waited there till we came to get them back!"

The harbour beach was a popular place for the children of the Beach Village. In this view, two Beach boys can be seen 'borrowing' one of the rafts which were used to paint the boats. No doubt they are keeping a watchful eye for Penny the policeman!

COASTGUARD STATION

HAMILTON DOCK

CRANE

JACKAMAN'S CORN

SHINGLE
MILL

BILLY
STONE'S
PIER

NORTH
PIER

ROYAL
PIER

LIFEBOAT
SHED WASHED
AWAY IN THE
1953 FLOOD

SOUTH
PIER

The Shingle Mill, in the centre of the photograph, on the North Extension.

Just before the Second World War the London North Eastern Railway decided to cash in on the vast amount of shingle which was accumulating on the North Extension. A vast screening plant was built, with massive timbers standing fifty feet high. A crane installed to scoop up the shingle dug out big holes in the sand which then filled up with water when the tide came in. The Beach boys used these as their very own swimming pools which they knew as the 'dykes'.

The dredging of shingle from the North Extension had been going on since the 1860s and many of the concrete roads which were laid around the town in the 1920s contained some of this natural material. However, after the Second World War the shingle was no longer so bountiful, and the North Extension itself began to show signs of erosion. In 1958 shingle extraction was finally halted. The vast screening plant remained though and became a playground for local lads, one of whom was tragically killed. Demolition was forthcoming and the landmark disappeared from the skyline in 1960.

The boys were certainly mischievous but strong discipline was always forth-coming as a result. Billy Keith remembers one incident when he climbed up on the roof of Sayer and Holloway's fish house, the place where his father worked as fore-man. " I climbed up and fell through the roof," recalls Billy, "and went straight into the red herrings. I had scales in my ears, up my nose and in my mouth, and they had to wash me down. But I had killed the dye, the pickle was broken, and they had to dump all those fish, the whole lot. My father, being in charge, really scalped me . . .!"

Ronny Wilson admits that he was always in trouble as a boy. "I was always get-ting wrong for something," he reveals, "like the time I had a stick, I made it myself, and when the man used to come along to light the lamps along the street, I put them all out, and he used to go round my father's house and say, 'Your bloody boy has put all the lamps out!' and I used to have to go round with my father and relight them and he'd give me a right clip over the head. Another time, I threw a stink bomb across the road to my mate, but as it went across the road Bingham's van went past and it went right in the window! My father had to pay for all the cakes and he gave me a clip around the ear, but it was accidental, I just threw it and it went straight in the window, bang! And then there was a big lorry there one day, with fifty pigs in it, and I just couldn't resist it, I just let the back down, and all the pigs went all round the roads, everywhere. Everyone was asking, 'Who let those pigs out?' but I never owned up. It took about six hours before they got them all back again!"

Charles Ellis recalls that there was briefly a salt factory near Ness Point, "When they cleared the site, they left the wall that went round the outside and that area was used for making Klondike boxes, big boxes to put the herring in. There was huge stacks of boxes on that site when it was cleared, thousands and thousands of boxes. The kids used to get in there then and make hides and tunnels through the boxes. After that the Scots girls had it for barrels but that factory stood empty for a while and as kids we were always getting in there. Near the chimney there was a huge wooden structure, which had a set of steps to the top where there were steel wires attached on each corner, running from the top down to the ground. We kids weren't really supposed to play on this thing and the police were always after us. One day we were on the top of the structure and three or four policemen came after us. They thought they'd got us, all they had to do was block these stairs. So a couple of them went upstairs after us, and do you know what we did? We all had cloth caps, so we put them round the wire and slid down it and ran away! We used to do that, slide down these wire guys. We were lucky really because the wire was years old and rusty, with pieces sticking out of it. If it went through your hat you would get it in your hand! And that was high too!"

Money was scarce and pocket money for children was mostly unheard of. If you wanted money, even as a child you had to work for it. Billy Keith says, "We used to sit down near the Coastguard and see the boats come round and say, so and so is on that boat, someone else is on that one, you go to that house, you go to that one, and we used to run to their house and tell them that their husbands were coming home and then we'd get treated. And then you'd go and tell the men as they were getting off the boats that we'd let their wives know and they'd treat us as well."

Ronny Wilson remembers, "I did some kitbagging before I was old enough to go to work, outside the Sparrow's Nest. With a barrow on the back of a bike, we used to carry twelve kit bags strapped up, roped up. I got a farthing once for taking some

The photograph shows the barrow boys opposite the main gate of the Sparrow's Nest. During the war years the boys used to cart the sailors' kit bags, charging threepence for trips north of the bridge and trying for sixpence south of it which they got if they were lucky.

to St. Lukes, a farthing! But usually you'd get a penny, or tuppence or sixpence. I got a quid for carrying one for a Scottish skipper from the bottom of the Ravine to the top once."

Bert Prettyman recalls some of the sporting activities. "We had a cricket pitch outside our house," he explains. "There was a telegraph pole there that we used to chalk the stumps on and our football pitch was Sharman's Opening. One side was the path, the other side was the wall. I wanted a pair of football boots badly and my mother said I can't afford to buy you any, you'll have to write to your brother Charlie. So I did, and I got them and so I was captain for the day in my brand new boots."

Ruby Timberley also remembers the boys playing football and cricket, ". . . with make-shift footballs and cricket balls and of course make-shift wickets and goal posts, but they still enjoyed their games. Some sat on pavements flicking playing cards or five flat stones. All harmless fun, keeping children out of mischief and costing nothing."

Ron James recollects that the Beach had its own Christmas traditions too. "For years I had my Christmas breakfast in the Beachmen's shed, but we were only allowed in there then, all the kids used to go down there. We never had Christmas trees, we had hoops. They used to have one hoop going one way and one going the other, tied in the middle, and then you put your crepe paper round that and decorated it with baubles and little bars of chocolate and hung it up in the window. We had our hoop made by my uncle because he was a cooper. That was our Christmas tree."

"Christmas morning, all the old boys used to walk round each other's and have a drink and then go into the next one. Well, that only went on till the pubs opened at twelve on Christmas Day, and then they'd start again and most likely finish up round one of them playing cards all of Christmas afternoon."

Eric Horne has his own memories of this time, "At Christmas, I remember puddings made and boiled in cloths for many hours in the brick copper or in large cast iron saucepans. I can't remember us having chicken for Christmas dinner, but a piece of roast pork was certainly a luxury. I recall Hannant's toy shop a little way down the High Street, where I would spend ages gazing through the window at the masses of toys mostly priced beyond the reach of Village people. However, with her hard work throughout the year, my mother made sure that we always had a good Christmas. One present I particularly remember was a metal van big enough to sit on, which I used to ride down from the top of the Score. I was sharply rebuked one day by a dear old lady in a Victorian bonnet. Rant Score was the only score wide enough for traffic and we did get the occasional vehicle or horse and cart passing through . . . In the summer, events took place on the old Battery Green, which was then a rough patch of grass in front of the Coastguard Cottages. One event featured men on horses, galloping around to the tune of 'All the king's horses and all the king's men'. The annual carnival route also went past here."

Mrs Hitter fondly remembers the Easters of her childhood, "Good Friday, Mother used to make the saffron buns, we used to call them saffron dingers . . . Mother used to give us a piece of bread and margarine and a hard boiled egg, marvellous to have an egg then, and we used to go on the Denes all day long, swing on them net posts, play on them, it was lovely. There was also a big fair down on the Beach when I was young, down Hamilton Road where the Scots girls used to have their barrels. Then there was May Day and the maypole. I used to love dressing up as the May Queen. My mother used to do my hair up in ringlets, a bit of curtain for a veil. We used to dress up in paper frocks, spend days making these paper frocks, and we all used to sing 'Climbin' up the walls, Knockin' down the spiders.' We used to go up to people's doors and sing and get pennies. We used to have a little tea party if we had enough."

Eric Horne continues, "On May Day, children would roam around together banging tins or saucepans, and chanting a ditty which went, 'Climbing up the walls, Knocking down the spiders, Cabbages and turnips too, Put them in your aluminium saucepan, And we'll have a rare old stew!' Children dressed up in old clothes, blackened their faces with burnt cork and walked round the streets after tea singing this song, which was sung to the tune of a Salvation Army hymn which started off with the words 'Turn to the Lord and seek salvation'. They knocked on doors, tin can in hand, for any small donations."

"The boys used to dress up in any old thing, and go about the Beach knocking on doors," says Matthew Boardley, "but one old girl in Old Nelson Street used to make us sing, 'Now is the month of May . . .' and we got money for that!"

Ethel Baker recalls singing that song too. "I remember May Day. We had a May Queen and about six others all dressed in paper dresses which we kids made and we sung 'Now is the month of May, when merry lambs are playing . . .' Then we had a tea party when the week was out."

"They were happy days," remembers Benny Knights, "because we had the whole of the Denes to play in." The Beach Village gave children freedom and a safe environment to live and play in, and was a community that gave them a feeling of security.

"We had such great fun," says Ronny Wilson, "so wonderful, it was the best part of my life, living down there."

*　　*　　*　　*

Beach boys on the pier. Left to right: Reggie Howe, Cecil Wilson, Freddie Wilson, George Wilson (lying down), Benny McNeil, Lenny Howe, Bobby Howe. George Wilson lived near Rist's, along Whapload Road whilst his cousin Cecil lived in Maltsters Score. Cecil remembers, "Like the kids take car numbers, we took boat numbers."

A Beach Boy's Lament

When we were a lot younger
we knew starvation and hunger.
We were all poor, yes, down and out,
if we were naughty, we got a good clout.
Mum was boss whilst Dad was at sea,
condensed milk sandwiches with sugar for tea.
We went to the bakers, and asked for stale buns
and off to the butchers for bones we did run.
A Sunday dinner we seldom had,
times I'm afraid were hard and very bad.
Second hand clothes were what we wore,
these had to last, as we got no more.
Holes in our shoes and down to the uppers,
we never worried about any suppers.
Down to the Market for an old cod's head,
this would be mixed with a swede and some bread.
Everything was asked for in hope of a meal
we were told always ask, never steal.

Travelling on trams we rolled shakily along
being so happy we could burst into song.
We played out in the streets for a bit of fun
and prayed overnight for a bright day and sun.
We played on the harbour beach, oh dear,
pinching a painter's raft, we knew no fear.
Playing on the beach and out on the street,
hopscotch, skipping, whip and top all were a treat
Marbles and glarnies, ciggies as well
tip cat, chase and tag, ring someone's bell.
We look back on memories, and also the past
knowing full well, they will always last.
The 'young uns' today don't know what life's like
with all their computers, TV and bikes.
We're getting older, oh yes, it is true
our days now are numbered and are nearly through.
Our time is drawing nearer every day,
remembering our past and how we used to play.
We had it rough, we had it good,
would we have had it better if we could?

The answer is yes, but what will be, will be.
I'm glad after all these years God made me, ME.

– Jack Rose –

Two views of the Coronation Day party at the Gas House Tavern, 2nd June 1953. The picture above was taken at the rear of pub and shows the fancy dress which is also captured in close up on the left.

The 'Gasworks Gang' as they were known, pictured here in 1956. Left to right, (top row) Valerie Harper, Jacqueline Jensen, Jean Hill, Denise Peters. (in front) Sadie Springer, Marlene Jensen, Sandra Coleman, Glennis Baldry, David Davis, Doris Davis, Leslie Harper.

Beach boys on the harbour beach with the drifter Boy George in the background.

6

Schools

*"Train up a child in the way he should go
and when he is old he will not depart from it."*

PROVERBS 22 VERSE 6

"Most of the children went to school with no boots or shoes," recalls Mr E. J. Day, who was born in 1903, "but each year before the bad weather the Parish used to send boxes of clogs to the school and if our mothers could afford it, we all got a pair for threepence a pair."

The children of the Beach Village were usually poor, and their life at school was a struggle. They were never far away from the hardships of their home life, and many can remember how every Friday afternoon the sons of the fishermen would be excused from lessons to go and get their fathers' wages from the company office to save the postage money.

There were a number of schools connected with the Beach Village, but after the First World War just three remained, Wilde's School, Mariners Score School and Central School. Previous to this there was also Annott's School, and Christ Church Infants, but the histories of all the schools in this area seem to overlap and some were amalgamated to add to the confusion.

Wilde's School was established as the result of a bequest from John Wilde, who stated in his will made on 22nd July 1735 that, after the death of his niece and housekeeper, Miss Smithson, part of his estate should be put in trust for the building of a school. This estate included dwelling houses, fish houses, yards and gardens in Lowestoft, and also land and property at Worlingham, all bequeathed by Wilde with the intention of opening a school for forty boys with a preference being given to the children of fishermen. The will also instructed that an annual sermon should be preached at the parish church of St. Margarets on the 23rd December, which was done for 150 years, the text being, "Train up a child in the way he should go and when he is old he will not depart from it".

John Wilde died in 1738, and upon the death of Miss Smithson (by then Mrs Perryson) on 7th December 1781, the trustees erected a building for a school in the score named after him according to his wishes. The original building was built in 1788 and the first master was Alexander Payne, who was appointed in 1790 to teach forty boys at this new free school which opened a year later. Another school room was built later at the bottom of Wilde's Score, which could be entered from Wilde's School playground. It seems likely this was constructed in 1831, as this date was marked out with the bottoms of dark bottles in the wall and this building became known as the 'Bottle Shed'. Charles Ellis recalls, "That held about twenty children

(Above)
The interior of the 'Bottle Shed' school room at Wilde's School, which later became Walter Larke's Hiker's Rest.

(Left)
Picture showing the date which was marked out in the wall with the bottom of dark bottles, situated on the gable end of the 'Bottle Shed'.

and the kids used to stand around a big cast iron stove which had a chimney through the roof. In the 1930s the school didn't use it any more and it became Walter Larke's billiard room and was called the Hiker's Rest."

George Osborne was born in 1911 and was a Wilde's School pupil between the ages of eight and fourteen, leaving in 1925. "In my day the 'Bottle Shed' was more or less for the first class and then you came up into the main building. I remember the toilets were outside in the playground. In the main building, where the three classes were, on the end wall it said 1788. Underneath was a clock and then there were these three nails on the wall with brass discs hanging from them and if you wanted to go to the toilet you had to take one of these with you. If there wasn't one there, you couldn't go, you had to wait for someone with a brass disc to come back."

"I never lived on the Beach but there were too many at the Church Road School, and so I went to Wilde's School. Amoss was headmaster then. When he came to school he had a cane up his sleeve. The teachers in my time were Mr Watson, Mr Regis, Mr Boswell, Mr Snelling and Amoss. My teacher was Mr Watson. During the school teachers' strike in 1923, we went to the camp at Oulton for 2/6d a week to be taught and we still had school every day!"

Among the headmasters at Wilde's School was William Douglas who held the position for twenty-four years until October 1892 when he was succeeded by George Arthur Amoss. In 1923, during the teachers' strike, Mr Brown took temporary charge of the school and in the mid-1920s, the long and strict reign of Mr Amoss finally ended when he presumably retired and was replaced by Charles Phillips, a keen cricketer. He stayed until 1936 when Wilde's became a mixed school and Miss F. Quintrell became headmistress. Benny Knights was born in 1909 and, like many of his generation, can vividly remember the notorious Mr Amoss. "He was a sod he was," recalls Benny, "I got three on each hand for fighting in the playground. He used to have a cane up his coat sleeve, and if you were marching into school he used to just slash you across the legs if you were out of step!"

Charles Ellis also has few fond memories of this headmaster, "Old Amoss, I was glad when I got away from him. I saw him one morning give thirty-six boys three cuts of the cane on each hand, he went through the whole lot and he never raised a sweat . . . There was one time when Amoss met his match though, and that was old Maud Wilson. She was a West Indian, about sixteen stone and built like Frank Bruno, with arms like tree trunks. Although she had a heart of gold, that old girl, she didn't stand no nonsense. She had a boy called Tommy. One day he'd done something wrong at school which upset Amoss and he came in there and he took Tommy out of the classroom. In the passage was a coffin-shaped box with a lid and all the waste paper used to go in there, and he put Tommy across it and all the boys in the class heard him, we counted the strokes, twenty-eight strokes. But Amoss made one mistake. When he finished, he let go of Tommy's collar, and he ran home. The next thing up came Maud. She'd got on a pair of men's leather sea boots and her apron and her sleeves rolled up. She came storming up there. Lynn Regis and Phillips were the masters there then and Phillips stood at the top of the steps at Wilde's School and all Maud said to him was, 'Where's Amoss?' and before he could answer she pushed him out the way, and he went straight down, flat on his back. And she looked in every class room, every cupboard, and behind every wall and desk. Do you know what the old beggar had done? Down the playground there was a little classroom on Whapload Road, it later became the Hiker's Rest, and there was a long narrow passage down there, and he went down there and hid behind that old stove. He must have seen her coming and realised what he'd done. She went through that school like a cyclone, I've never seen anything like it, she was absolutely boiling, steam coming out of her ears. All she could say was, 'Where's Amoss?' and the other teachers wouldn't go near her. 'Where's Amoss? WHERE'S AMOSS?' And I do believe to this day, if she had caught Amoss at that time she would have killed him. She would. Of course, she couldn't find him so she went home and she must have cooled off. She was like a man gone mad though. I've never seen a woman like it!"

Discipline was strict, although not all punishment came in the form of the cane. "The school had an allotment near St. Margaret's School," explains Charles Oldman, "and if you were a bad boy, you got put on the allotment detail and spent all day weeding!" Charles was at Wilde's School during Mr Phillip's tenure as headmaster and although he was only there a year he can vividly recall that time. He can especially remember playing Wilde's cricket, a game unique to Wilde's School. "We used to have a sloping playground," he says, "and we played this cricket on there, with stumps in the four corners and if you were facing the bowler, bowling down hill, you knew it!"

"I used to play Wilde's cricket," Leonard Boyce recalls, "Because the school was built in the score the playground was on a slope at the back of the school, and we used to have stumps in four corners and four batsmen and fielders in the middle and bowl from end to end . . . this game was mainly Mr Regis's doing, he was very keen on sport. He was eventually chairman of Lowestoft Town Football Club." Mr Boyce can also remember playing standard cricket. "Phillips was headmaster in my day, and he was captain of Lowestoft cricket team. He used to march us up to Corton Road playing fields once a week in the summer, and most of the time we spent bowling to him, give him practice for Saturday. I always remember he used to put his pads on and say, 'I'll show you how to bat, boys!' "

Leonard went to Wilde's School in 1926, after going to Arnold Street School and St. Margaret's. "It wasn't a very large school," he recalls, "and I can remember the names of the teachers. The headmaster was a Mr Phillips, the senior teacher was Mr Lynn Regis, a very nice man, then there was a Mr Taylor but I was never taught by him, a Mr Bull and Mr Boswell. I don't think there were any more down there, but they all ruled with a rod of iron, and they were all good teachers. I finished up with Mr Regis in what they used to call the top class, which amounted to the class you were in before you left school at fourteen. I was very fond of Mr Regis, he was strict but very fair and he used to stand very straight, a very proud man he was. He'd been in the army in the First World War, and he used to tell us tales about that in school. He used to have a stick, two or three feet long, and though I never saw him hit anyone with it, he used to smash it upon the desk if anyone was misbehaving or anything like that."

"At Wilde's School I saw several children who came to school with no shoes or socks on, just bare feet, and he used to speak about it, did Mr Regis, but he never pursued it because he knew the poor devils didn't have any money to buy them. And though some of the children were a bit rough and ready, he had them under his thumb, he was a very good teacher."

In the mid-1930s Wilde's School became a mixed school with Mr Phillips leaving the post of headmaster and Miss Quintrell taking over. Joy Pearce remembers, "I went to Arnold Street School first, then I went to Wilde's Score School where

66

Wilde's School pupils pictured in the sloping playground. This was where their own form of cricket was played, known as Wilde's cricket. Charles Oldman recalls, "... If you were facing the bowler, bowling down hill, you knew it! ..."

In 1923 Wilde's School pupils were being taught at the St. Margaret's Institute during the teachers' strike. George Osborne is in the second row, fourth from the right, and he recalls, "... During the school teachers' strike we went to the camp at Oulton for 2/6d a week to be taught and we had school every day ..." The notorious Mr Amoss is on the right of the photograph.

Mr Boswell was my teacher. Then the war came along and I had a break from school as my grandmother wouldn't let me be evacuated so I stopped at home."

Wilde's School closed at the start of the Second World War and never re-opened. Most of the school's buildings were destroyed during World War II, but the remaining Victorian structure was leased to the newly established John Wilde Club in 1948, which was a sort of social club. Club members refurbished the building and during this work they found the date slab from the original building which was inscribed '1788'. The club moved from these premises at the end of the 1970s and on the 8th February 1980 the building was bought by Birds Eye Foods and was used for their personnel training rooms and later as a store room for staff archives. In 1995 Birds Eye asked Waveney District Council if they wanted the property, and the Lowestoft Civic Society were approached to see if they could find a use for the old building. Since then work has begun on refurbishment with the intention of turning the building into a Heritage Centre.

On 12th May 1943 Wilde's School was bombed. This photograph shows the devastation looking from Whapload Road towards the High Street. The school had closed at the beginning of the war and was being used as the headquarters of the Lowestoft Air Training Corps. The building in the centre of the photograph, which was part of Wilde's School, is currently being renovated.

The history of Wilde's School shows links with Annott's school, which was the oldest school in the town, established in the 1500s with money bequested by Thomas Annott. Originally situated in the Town Close next to St. Margaret's Church, in 1674 this building became so dilapidated that the school moved to the Town Chamber over the Corn Cross. In the first half of the nineteenth century, Annott's School moved to a building east of Flint House, which we suppose was at the top end of Wilde's Score, where pupils received instruction under John Salmon and Samuel Chambers. This building was enlarged in 1843.

In 1872, with both schools in Wilde's Score, it was suggested that they should be amalgamated and move to Beccles Road in Oulton Broad, presumably on land which was part of John Wilde's bequest. However the idea never came to fruition, and in 1883 Annott's School moved from Wilde's Score and united with the

National School in Mariners Score, although the Annott name was retained until the last years of the nineteenth century, when it became known as Mariners Score School. It seems there had been a school in Mariners Score since the mid-1800s. This appears to have been established by the Rev. F. Cunningham, who in 1830 started building the first of his three schools in the north of the town. One of these was the Great Girls' School in Mariners Score, and it seems likely that this was the Mariners Score School referred to in the 1902 Kelly's Directory as being built in 1846 for 182 children. In 1877 the Boys' National School moved to Mariners Score, from their building which would become the Convalescent Home opposite Belle Vue Park, now Abigail Court, and presumably joined with the girls' school already at Mariners Score. Now this became known as St. Margaret's National School. In 1883 the National School was amalgamated with Annott's, who moved from Wilde's Score. With Mr E. Atkins as master, and Miss Hubbard as mistress, this newly combined school took the name of Annott's. By 1901 this school had simply become known as Mariners Score School and had 181 pupils with Mr Atkins remaining the Head until 1914 when the schools in the area were reorganised. Christ Church Infants School was situated at the bottom of Herring Fishery Score in premises which were built in 1892, currently part of Christ Church Hall.

In 1914 this school, with Mr Atkins as master, moved into the new Whapload Road Council School which had just been built and would later become the Central School when the schools were re-structured again in 1919. It was then that this new school was upgraded and the infants school moved from here into the old Mariners Score School building, becoming known as Mariners Score Infants, under the headship of Miss Ethel Strickland. In 1974, Beatrice Hardingham, one of the teachers at this school, wrote a letter to the Lowestoft Journal which included some interesting details of the time she spent working there. She wrote, ". . . Miss Strickland, Miss Hook and I all taught in the same long room in that school (there were about 100 children). Our classes were separated by a curtain, and two shoulder-high screens. The youngest children occupied the small room at the rear of the building and their teacher was Miss Walker. We went to Mariners Score School supposedly for three years, but remained there 15 years until it was finally closed in 1934. Miss Strickland was transferred to Morton Road School, Miss Hook to Lovewell Road School and I went to Lovewell Road Junior School. In spite of working in such difficult conditions, we had some happy and amusing times."

Mrs Timberley went to Mariners Score School in the 1920s–30s, "My brothers, sister and myself were all born in the Beach Village, and lived there until about 1941. We all attended Mariners Score School as infants. We had teachers who were strict, kind and dedicated. We could all read and write by the age of six years and could repeat most of the tables. At the age of eight years we moved on to other schools. We had prayers at the beginning of the day and before we went home in the afternoon. We also sang the hymn, 'Now the day is over.' We had a good grounding and were disciplined."

"I went to school at Mariners Score," recalls Ron James. "Miss Strickland was the headmistress and she was something strict! One of the things we used to do on the way to school was after the Scots girls had filled the barrels with herring. They used to put the brine in and just tap the cork in because after a while the fish soaked up the brine so they used to fill up before they shipped them to Russia or wherever. Before they put the bungs tight in, we used to run along there to school and we used

Miss Hook's class at Mariners Score School in 1927. Charles Oldman can be seen third from the left in the top row.

Miss Hardingham's class at Mariners Score School in 1931. Bert Prettyman, who can be found far right on the bottom row, organises the Beach reunions which have proved so popular in recent years.

Mariners Score School closed in 1934. It seems likely that this was originally the Great Girls' School, built in 1846 for 182 children, before going through various amalgamations until it was finally simply known as Mariners Score School by the early 1900s.

to kick the barrels and if you weren't quick enough the brine would go all over you or the boy running behind you! When you went into school at Mariners Score, they used to have those tortoise stoves, they used to get red hot and if you sat near them after you did that, it would really stink of fish! And Miss Strickland would come along and she used to clip you across the lug and tell you to go home and change! Of course, you had nothing to change into!"

Charles Oldman remembers, "I was about three years old when we left my mother's parents' and rented a cottage, if you could call it that, in a block called Scarle's Buildings, which was at the back of Mariners Score School. If you went down Mariners Score you came to the school and there was a little gate and a passageway, and you turned left and there was a row of cottages which as I said ran parallel with the score and you also approached them from the bottom where now Waveney Tyres are. In fact, nothing remains there now . . . I was four years and five months when I went to Mariners Score School which was out of the cottage, just up the passage and you were there. There were only three classes there and three teachers. Miss Strickland, who was the headmistress, and Miss Hook and Miss Hardingham. Mariners Score was like a primary school. After I was about seven and a half I went up to St. Margaret's School and from there I went for about a year to Wilde's School . . . when I was ten and a half I got a scholarship to Lowestoft Central School."

Lowestoft Central School was opened in 1919 in the former Whapload Road School which had been built in 1914 at a cost of £6,800. Three hundred pupils were admitted to the new school, entrance to which was by scholarship only. Mr T. H. Adams, M.B.E. was the only headmaster of the school for its brief thirty year history, during which time it gained an excellent reputation. The pupils were proud to wear their uniforms and display the yellow and black badge. Known as 'Plummy', the nickname derived from one of the town's Mayors by the same name who was a greengrocer, Mr Adams was well thought of by his pupils and everyone who can recall him seems to hold him in high regard. He was considered to be both a good headmaster and a kind and generous man too. Although Jack Rose never went to Central School, he has his own recollection of Plummy Adams. When Jack was a young boy, his back gate opened out into Herring Fishery Score and he often sat on the back step watching the older children going to school. Sitting there with his backside out of his trousers, clothes torn and dirty through playing in the fish yards, perhaps you would think no-one would have time for this ragamuffin. However, Mr Adams always stopped and asked, 'How's my little man today?' Jack didn't know who he was until several years later but it always stuck in his mind, those words and kind attention meaning a lot to a youngster in those days.

Whapload Road School was built in 1914, the building later housing the Central School. The headmaster of this mixed infants school was Mr Atkins who had previously been the head at Mariners Score School, and this photograph shows one of the first intakes of pupils around the time of the school's opening.

Among the first teachers at Central School in 1919 were Miss Cecily Rhodes, the senior mistress, Miss Ethel Howden, Miss Rose Monk, Miss Alison Penzer, Mr Percy Blake, Mr C. W. E. Todd, Mr Fred Wales and Mr Fred Moore. Charles Oldman can remember some of the later teachers at the Central School, ". . . Mr Wilkin was the history and maths teacher, the art master was Arthur Gooch, Miss Spadham was an English teacher, Miss Gibson was music, Herbie Bushell was geography, Oscar Outlaw was woodwork and metalwork, and 'Fiddler' Moore, he used to play the violin, he was the science teacher. When I was at Central School the tuck shop of the school was Squire's shop."

"Central School had two floors with long corridors, classrooms each side, a big hall down the bottom, and on the top floor on the left was the headmaster. There were about twelve classrooms there. The teachers taught their subject throughout the school, like Wilkin would be taking maths and history but he would be teaching forms three, four, five and six. You had a form classroom but for every lesson there would be an allotted classroom. So if you had English, you went to the English classroom. The teachers didn't move, you went to them . . . I should have stayed at Central School until I was fifteen, it was one of the conditions of the school, so when I was fourteen I had to go before the full Education Committee in the town hall to get released from school because I had a job lined up."

to the Central School and I was there till about 1932 . . . The Central School was the first to serve school dinners. Miss Grieg used to cook the meal and it was sold to some of the pupils, the boys from Lound and places like that. The rest of them as I remember used to go down Hammond's fish and chip shop."

All the schools on the Grit closed at the beginning of the war because of the evacuation. Initially, Central School was used by servicemen as accommodation during the hostilities but during an air raid on 13th June 1941 at 3.45 a.m. the school received a direct hit and thirteen servicemen and one civilian were killed. Although the Central School was destroyed, three separate classrooms along Herring Fishery Score, the science laboratory, the woodwork room and the cookery room survived and after the war became part of the Navigation School. Many of the former pupils of Central School perished during this war too. Charles Ellis continues, ". . . There were thirty-two boys in my class. Times were bad in the 1930s, and there was no work and Mr Adams told us that the Royal Air Force were recruiting for air crews. You had to pass an entrance exam but at least it would be a career and about twenty of the thirty-two volunteered for the Royal Air Force. There was so many of them that they allowed a room to be put aside at Central School and they took the exam there. They all passed I think and, of course, when the war broke out, they were all trained air crew, and if I look back at my class sixteen were killed in the Air Force."

After the war, none of the schools in the Beach Village re-opened, the buildings being either demolished or put to a variety of other uses. The children were sent up into the town for their schooling, and another part of the Grit's sense of community and independence was lost.

✳   ✳   ✳   ✳

The pupils of Central School photographed in 1935.

Picture continued over next two pages

Central School teachers, 1935, Mr Gooch, Miss Wilson, Mr Bushell, Miss Kitson, Mr Moore, Miss Badham, Mr Adams (Headmaster), Miss Howden, Mr Outlaw, Miss Craig, Mr Wilkin, Miss Needham.

◀ *Built in 1914, this school became known as the Central School in 1919. ". . . Central School had two floors with long corridors," remembers Charles Oldman, "classrooms each side, a big hall down the bottom, and on the top floor on the left was the headmaster. There were about twelve classrooms there . . ." Christchurch Hall can be seen on the left.*

The Central School was bombed on 13th June 1941 at 03.45 hours. At the time the building was being used as accommodation for service-men and fourteen soldiers and one civilian were killed, one body being blown up into Ayers' pigeon loft at the rear of 104 High Street.

Class 1, Mariners Score Infants School (as it became in 1919) in 1924. Miss Strickland can be seen standing to the left.

7

The Most Easterly Parish

"Not that there shall be wrecks,
but if there are, that they may be on our beach."

THE BEACHMEN'S PRAYER

"We went morning, afternoon and evening to Christ Church," says Hazel Boardley, "and at 8 o'clock used to have an open air meeting down there. I was a teenager then, and we had a little old organ, which we called Wheezy-Anna, and we all used to gather round this lamp-post and have an open air meeting. As soon as they heard the music all the cottage doors would open and the ladies would all come and lean on their doorposts and listen to our meeting. And that was called the 'halleluja' lamp-post."

Although situated as Crowe's Handbook puts it, ". . . among that class of inhabitants who are generally least disposed to go in quest of religious instruction . . ." there have always been places of worship in this area. One of the earliest of these was a Primitive Methodist chapel which could be found near the bottom of Denny's Score (now Wilde's Score) in the early 1800s, and there was also a Ranters' Chapel situated in the area where Coleman Square was later built.

The North Beach Bethel was situated in East Street at the bottom of Rant Score East between Whapload Road and the gasworks. Its establishment in the early 1900s owed much to the persistence and efforts of Mr A. G. Boyd, who purchased property in Beach Street (which later became East Street) and Anguish Street, entirely at his own cost, for the site of the Bethel. There were difficulties initially in obtaining the site as the old cooperage building standing there had been let to J. Grieve and Son but apparently as soon as they heard what the purpose of Mr Boyd's purchase was 'they came forward with the greatest kindness and accepted space found for them on another part of the property.' The site was cleared and the corner stone was laid on July 10th 1902. Two hundred people attended the opening service on September 4th 1902 and the Bethel continued until the Second World War, Mrs Boyd becoming Superintendent after her husband's death in 1922. A stone scroll was erected in his memory outside the North Beach Bethel and it can currently be found outside the Battery Green Bethel.

The plans for Christ Church were drawn up during a religious revival by the Rev. Francis Cunningham shortly before his death on 13th August 1863. Cunningham was the rector of Pakefield from 1815 to 1855 and vicar of Lowestoft between 1830 and 1860, and it was he who started a collection for the construction of the church and the endowment of the new vicarage at the end of 1862 with the Bishop of the Diocese among the first of the contributors. Christ Church was built for the

Christ Church opened on February 12th 1869 and was originally called the Cunningham Memorial Beachmen's Church for the Beachmen and Fishermen of Lowestoft.

The Primitive Methodist Chapel along Whapload Road was one of the earliest places of worship on the Beach. The building was there before 1863 and was closed when the Methodists built their new chapel in St. Peter's Street in 1876. During World War One it was used as a soup kitchen and after the Second World War Birds Eye had the building for their sanitation store. It was demolished in January 1968.

ever-increasing residents of the Beach Village, giving them their own minister and church and confirming them as a parish of their own.

Three thousand people attended the stone laying ceremony which was a festive occasion. The weather was said to have been 'splendidly fierce' and the scaffolding, flagstaffs and the houses displayed a 'profusion of flags and banners'. This stone was placed at the south east corner of the tower and had the following inscription which is now illegible:

This First Stone
of
Christ Church Lowestoft
Erected to the Glory of God and in the memory of the
Rev. Francis Cunningham M.A. R.D.
was laid on 4th day of May 1868 by the Rev. William Nottridge Ripley. M.A.

W. Oldham Chambers   Jackson and Rounce
   Architect   Builders

When the new church, built in the Early English style and seating about four hundred and sixty, opened on February 12th 1869, it was called the Cunningham Memorial Beachmens Church for the Beachmen and Fishermen of Lowestoft. The first incumbent was the Rev. E. J. Barnes (1867–1878), who before the Church was opened gave Bible classes and started a Sunday School in his front room for young lads. The Rev. Barnes soon became involved in community life in the Beach Village and if the maroons were fired to call out the lifeboat during a service, every one including the vicar left the church to help launch the lifeboat, continuing the service on their return.

The villagers signed a pledge to 'follow the Lord's example and be present at the services in our Father's House on His day unless prevented by a good reason that could be conscientiously given to our Lord and Saviour, the head of the Church'. To further encourage the residents the church wardens were instructed that the hiring of 'sittings' (the reserving of pews) should be exclusive to the inhabitants of the Beach Village and the rent therefore be low.

Christ Church always tried to relieve the poverty of the surrounding community such as in February 1895 when in one week between five and six thousand poor hungry children were provided with free breakfasts in Christ Church School Room (which had been opened in 1892) at a cost of a pound per two hundred children. When the church was opened in 1869 it was chronically short of money and was unable to raise £500 for the consecration. Thirty years later Christ Church still hadn't been able to scrape the money together and the Bishop agreed to waive this requirement. The western aisles and the church organ were not added to the church until later and the clock was installed on June 15th 1901 when a generous parishioner, Mr Slipper Barnes, who lived in Old Nelson Street, paid £120 for the timepiece. However, due to the church's financial restrictions they were unable to pay for the upkeep of the clock and the town council agreed to take over the financial responsibilties of the maintenance. A Mr J. Bonsall was appointed to wind and regulate it for the sum of £4 a year, although there was some difficulty handing it over as a public clock since it had been a private gift. This was overcome by drawing up an agreement under which the council had the right of entry to the church. The council was also granted the right to light, wind and repair the clock and have done so until recently, when they decided that this requirement was now defunct, as public clocks are not so important due to the fact that wrist-watches are so widely used.

One of the happiest times in Christ Church's history was in March 1921, when a religious revival began in Lowestoft under the preaching of the Rev. A. Douglas Brown from Balham, London. The first meetings were at London Road Baptist Church and the Fishermen's Bethel, Battery Green which were packed for every service. After the first week it was decided to hold afternoon Bible readings at Christ Church. The first one filled the Parish Room, the next one filled the church, and so it continued for three weeks, including Easter week and on Good Friday, in spite of services in other churches, Christ Church was more crowded than ever. On those afternoons the trams were full of people carrying Bibles, and the conductor would call out, "Get off here for Christ Church," as they reached Old Nelson Street.

The vicar of Christ Church at the time, Rev. John Hayes, wrote about this experience in March 1921, saying, "I want to take you into my church one Wednesday evening. At a quarter to seven the church is full, it is 'bung' full and I have to go up in the pulpit and say to the people, 'My friends, I want those of you who love the Lord Jesus to go out. I want you to go into the Parish Hall and pray.' They got up and went, here and there all over the church; they passed into the Parish Hall, some two hundred of them gathered there, and they held a prayer meeting. Then I had to say to the young men, 'I want you to get up and sit on the floor at the front': and we had to get people into that church packed in that way, and in the vestry. In the Parish Hall they were praying; there was a sister praying for her sister who was in the church, and at the close of the service that sister came to me and said, 'I want to talk to you'. On the following Tuesday evening that sister was led to Christ in my study in answer to the prayer offered in the Parish Hall."

Two of Christ Church's longest serving parishioners are Matthew and Hazel Boardley who both grew up on the Beach, and were married in the church in 1939. Matthew was born in 1916 and grew up more or less next door to the church, at 1 Jubilee Terrace. From the age of three he was in the Sunday School class, moving on to the Boys' Brigade and becoming a Sunday School teacher. ". . . I missed out on the choir though," explains Matthew, "because I couldn't stand the stiff shirt collars you had to wear!" In 1956 Matthew became the first Beach boy to be made churchwarden, although this was on a temporary basis, a 'temporary' period which lasted 23 years until he retired in May 1979 and was succeeded by Derek Bacon.

Hazel was born in 1918 and lived opposite the *Rising Sun* public house and she too went to Christ Church from an early age. "My mother was a Methodist but sent us to Christ Church because it was the best Sunday School . . . Up in the High Street, Porter had a bakers shop and a cake shop but behind, running down into Crown Score, there was this wide stretch of garden, apple trees, flowers and all sorts and we used to hire this at Christ Church for a tennis club . . . Then there was the Sunday School treat. They used Pretty's coal carts as Mr Pretty was a Superintendent at the Sunday School. Mostly we used to go to Boardley's Meadow, which was to do with the other side of Matthew's family. The meadow was at Normanhurst, where the fire station is now but we also went to Hopton and Beccles, places like that."

Ruby Timberley went to Sunday School at Christ Church in the 1920s, "We were christened when we were babies in long clothes. When we were about three or four years old we started to attend Sunday School. Our teacher at this early age was a

Christ Church and Whapload Road. In the distance the Primitive Methodist Chapel can be seen.
Christ Church was at the centre of Beach Village life and most of the children born in this area went
to Sunday School either here or at the Bethel.

The 'halleluja' lamp-post on the junction of Anguish Street and Wilde's Street where parishioners from
Christ Church gathered for open air meetings. The cottages are 25, 27, 29 and 31 Anguish Street and
Daisy Dinks is said to have lived along this row.

Miss Spurgeon, who was related to Mr Spurgeon, the coxswain of the lifeboat at that time. The room where we were taught was very bare. There was a wooden floor, no mats, and there were two long forms down the middle of this room on which we all sat, our feet not touching the floor. We were not allowed to speak unless spoken to. If we did not pay attention to what Miss Spurgeon was trying to teach us she would lift us up and bang our bottoms on the form."

Ron James also remembers Miss Spurgeon, "I used to go to Sunday School there and Albert Spurgeon, the coxswain of the lifeboat, had a sister who used to be the Sunday School teacher. She weighed about sixteen stone and if you didn't behave yourself or you got caught talking she used to shake you up and down."

Mrs Timberley continues, "One Sunday afternoon each summer all the Sunday School children marched along Whapload Road following the Boys' Brigade Band and the Christ Church banner on the occasion of our Sunday School anniversary. Of course we always had what was called the Sunday School treat. This took place on a Thursday afternoon which at that time was early closing day and some of the teachers worked in shops. The venue in the 1920s was the Crown Meadow. The older children and teachers, also helpers, walked behind the church banner but the infants were transported in Mr J. Pretty's coal carts. Mr O. Pretty was our Sunday School Superintendent so he made sure that the carts were scrubbed out, with clean sacks put on the seats. It was a great occasion for us – the highlight of our summer."

"We were all dressed in our Sunday best and some of us had button-holes of sweet-peas provided by aunties. Mums and grannies came to wave us off as the band started up. We were so excited we could have been in a Rolls-Royce. Mums and grannies joined us later and joined in the fun, games and races, and of course, tea with two kinds of slab cake. There was always someone with a large tin of sweets which were thrown into the air for us to scramble for. We all went home tired out!"

"I can remember the Sunday School treats," says Mrs Jessie Hitter, "they used Pretty's coal carts, scrubbed out with clean sacks on the floor and all the kids used to get in there. We used to go as far as Carlton and think we were right out in the country. We played games in a field and had our tea which was potted meat sandwiches and a little bit of cake and we used to run around the field and have about threepence to spend which was a lot of money in those days. We used to buy flowers for our mothers but they'd be dead before we got them home. We'd have a ha'penny cornet. Our mothers used to come and see us off in the cart with our nice little frocks and hats."

Many of the Beach children joined the 'Young Harvesters' club which was held above Christ Church school room. Mrs Wright was the lady in charge in the 1920s, and there were magic lantern shows once a week and other events. The North Beach Bethel also ran a Sunday School, and this too proved popular. In 1912 the Bethel's Sunday School had fifteen teachers and a Superintendent, and about a hundred and twenty-five children attended each Sunday, and a hundred and ten of these earned prizes.

"I went to Sunday School in the little Bethel," says John 'Rhubarb' Gurney, "There was Sister Nell and Mr Wylie, they were the teachers. Of course, a lot of the boys would only turn up when the treats were on, but they didn't seem to mind."

Amongst Jean Mitchell's earliest recollections are, ". . . going to Sunday School at the Little Bethel where Sister Nell and Gwenny Nunn taught us our scriptures. We used to have Sunday School treats and once a year if you had very good attendance you received a prize. Every week you received a small printed text."

The North Beach Bethel was in East Street at the bottom of Rant Score East, between Whapload Road and the gasworks. Written in the stone over the door of the building was, 'Christ Jesus came into the world to save sinners' and underneath this was, 'Ever reconciled to God'.

The establishment of the Bethel on the Beach was largely due to Mr Alexander Gaviller Boyd, pictured above right, who purchased the land it was built on entirely at his own expense. Mr Boyd died in 1922 and a stone scroll was erected in his memory outside the North Beach Bethel which can now be seen outside the Seamen's Bethel in Battery Green Road.

The interior of the Bethel. The building held two hundred and the opening service was held on September 4th 1902.

"I went to the Little Bethel's Sunday School," says Charles Ellis, "you had a blue card and every time you went you got a stamp, which was a little star, and if you got fifty-two stars you were given a book to keep, something like 'Treasure Island'. You were something proud of that! I had three or four prizes."

The North Beach Bethel closed at the beginning of the Second World War and never re-opened. Christ Church however is still standing, having not only survived the war and the demolition of its surrounding parish, but also the flood which engulfed the area on the night of January 31st, 1953. "There had been floods before," explains Matthew Boardley, "but the 1953 flood was different, a wall of water swept down Whapload Road. If Christ Church had a door facing north when that flood water came down, we'd have had a lot more water in the church. The way Christ Church was built meant that it didn't affect it much. Most of it was in the aisles and we could just sweep it out."

The Rev. Peter Street was the vicar at the time, and was having a bath that evening at the vicarage when the phone rang. "It was around 10.30," he told Royal Flaxman for his book *Wall of Water* in 1993. "I answered the phone and it was the police with disturbing news. 'Your church is under water!' they told me. 'You'd better come quick!' I made a hasty finish to my bath and arrived at the church shortly before 11 p.m. to find that the church was indeed under water." That night the Rev. Street was one of the many that worked tirelessly against the flood, with the vicarage opening its doors to twenty-four people left homeless by the sudden surge of water. By morning Rev. Street was tired and filthy, and while he was standing on the back of a lorry travelling up the High Street he began to see members of his congregation walking to the church, completely unaware of any flood. "I was quite surprised when I realised it was already time for morning service, and there was even more surprise on their faces at seeing their vicar standing on the back of a lorry, as black as a coalman!"

With around eight per cent of the Church's parish flooded, immediate action was necessary and the next day Christ Church Hall was opened to provide food and clothing for flood victims. The Rev. Peter Street remembers, "Through the agony and damage caused to many homes we were able to bring Christian help to many people. Some of the fisher folk and members of the congregation also gave many hours of their time. The flood brought people together in the weeks following as never before."

In 1967 there were proposals put forward to close Christ Church and amalgamate with St. Peter's Church in the town. Although Christ Church had lost most of its parish by this time, the church's congregation was growing due to an influx of people from a wider area. "The congregation now come from all over the place," says Hazel Boardley. "We haven't got a parish like we used to have, our parish is up the town now. The church is now in the middle of an industrial area. We all descend in cars, we come from all over." As a result of this it was St. Peter's Church which was closed and demolished, and its organ relocated in Christ Church.

Matthew and Hazel Boardley's long involvement with Christ Church is only surpassed by George Francis who is now the church's longest serving parishioner. George, who was also the church verger for nearly forty years, was born and bred in the Beach Village, "My father worked in a fish house, he was a 'smoker', then he went and worked for Jewson's. We lived at 5 Rant Score East, near Binks' Bakery and I went to Wilde's School, it was called Wilde's Endowed then if you please! When I left school I was a cooper at Sayer and Holloway for a time till I left there and went to Jewson's until my retirement but I left the Beach when I got married and moved up into the town to Crown Street. Christ Church has been my life though, really. I was a choir boy, Sunday School teacher, Bible class leader, officer in the Boys' Brigade. I got married there, and was verger there for nearly forty years. My wife was a Sunday School teacher there too. I've been at Christ Church since I was three years old, and I am now ninety! Yes, it's been my life."

*   *   *   *

Vicars of Christ Church

E. J. Barnes 1867–1878

J. Lancaster 1878–1883

E. W. S. Kingdom 1883–1890

D. Dickson 1890–1912

A. Hewitt 1912–1918

J. Hayes 1918–1923

J. A. G. Ainley 1923–1928

E. Morris-Jones 1928–1933

T. Bragg 1934–1937

V. L. Treanor 1937–1946

H. Sutton 1946–1952

P. E. Street 1952–1957

R. H. Smith 1957–1967

E. P. Rudman 1967–1973

P. J. Bye 1973–1980

R. J. Payn 1981–1992

P. Moon 1994–

Christ Church is now the most easterly church in the British Isles, despite the fact that its surrounding parish gradually disappeared after the Second World War. ". . . The congregation now come from all over the place . . ." says Hazel Boardley.

8

'The Village Shops

"... I lived on Whapload Road, at 2 Canary Cottages,
next door to Mr Burwood's grocery shop. He sold almost
all and everything in that tiny cramped shop, and had a slate
where you paid for items when you had the money ..."
JOHN DAY

The shops on the Grit were humble affairs, small, family-run businesses, but they gave the area an independence as nearly any item could be purchased from these shops, from muffins to paraffin. There was no need to visit the town; the Beach was a self-contained community.

"Milk came to the doorstep like it does today," says Ruby Timberley, "but it was sold from a big milk churn on the back of a pony and trap." This was delivered by Joseph Flertey, who was the milkman on the Beach and had premises at 89 Whapload Road. However, you could also buy milk elsewhere on the Beach, as Mrs Timberley recalls, "There was a dairy (milk only) at the bottom of Old Nelson Street owned by two sisters, the Misses Bishop. Their milk was in large china bowls covered with net cloths, you took your mother's jug to buy milk."

Leonard Adams, also remembers Joseph Flertey, "He would come up Maltsters Score and ask us lads to look after his float while he went round the houses. When he came back he would ask one of us to take a few bottles down to the shop and he would give us a ha'penny. This went on for months and we thought we were helping until I heard my mother thanking him. It was just a way of him helping us lads as when he came up the score he was only twenty yards off the dairy shop."

In the late 1920s when Joseph Flertey moved away from the Beach to premises in the town, his old shop was acquired by Godfrey 'Maggot' Girling. "... I had my first barber shop on the Beach Village where old Flertey's dairy used to be," explains Godfrey. "I rented it for about six bob a week, something like that. This was in the days when I used to charge fourpence, or threepence for boys. I was there three or four years till I moved to 8 Whapload Road, near Fletcher's bicycle shop where I was for about five years until I joined up in January 1940."

Godfrey had begun his career at the age of eleven, working in Crown Street as a lather boy at Albert Hawk's. He went from there to Jack Blowers in Commercial Road for four years. He recalls, "He used to go for his dinner at one o'clock, and he wouldn't come back until four. There was me going like hell, it was a busy shop, and so I say to him, 'Look here Jack, I do all this work, I want a ten bob a week rise.' He say, 'I can't afford that,' so I say, 'All right, I'm packing up Saturday night and going to start up on the Beach.' I had it all planned and that's when I went down there, the last day in the old year, 1929."

Like most of the shops on the Beach Village, one of Godfrey's busiest times was during the autumn herring fishing season, "I went down there one Saturday morning during the fishing time. Quarter to eight I started working and I didn't finish there till ten past nine in the evening, and I didn't have a drink or anything, didn't stop. When I counted my money up, do you know how much I took? Thirty-four shillings and ninepence! I thought to myself, that doesn't seem very much, but then I sat and thought, them poor old buggers who work for Boardley only get thirty four bob a week. I earned that in a day so I couldn't complain, could I ?"

When Godfrey used to ask his customers, 'Do you want anything on your head?' he often used to get the reply, 'Shove some Yarmouth oil on.' This puzzled him as he'd never heard of Yarmouth oil, so one day he asked one of his customers and was told that it related to the fishing. It seems that the old fishermen used to wear leather boots and to soften theirs the Lowestoft men used oil. However, the Yarmouth men used to tow their boots behind their boats when steaming, so what Yarmouth oil amounted to was water!

Some people couldn't afford haircuts though, and many children had to make do with the pudding basin over the head for Mum or Dad to cut round. "Times were very hard for most families and also for some tradesmen. Money was very short," recalls Mrs Timberley, "and the tradesmen needed your custom and in most cases went out to get it. I remember a Mr Gray who had a bake house on Whapload Road, quite near the church. It may have been him who came round on Sunday mornings selling hot muffins in time for breakfast. He always looked as if he had been in a flour bag himself. He would cook cakes or joints for families. Another man came round ringing a bell on Sunday afternoons selling freshly boiled shrimps."

"The butcher and baker came delivering on trade bikes with the little front wheel," recalls John Day, "and they carried a wickerwork basket and all goods for sale were inside the basket. A man who sharpened knives and grass shears also visited now and again. As did a chap selling paraffin from a huge drum drawn by a horse. 'Tinks' or Romanies also did running repairs during the year and fixed kettles and enamel basins and sold clothes pegs, washing cloths and wooden utensils."

". . . Between the wars my father George kept a shoe repair shop on the Beach at 8 Anguish Street," remembers John Buck. "It was a house converted into a shop with two rooms downstairs and one upstairs. He used to mend the shoes in one room and in the other room he had a big finishing machine. You used to open the door, go in, and he had a counter along one side and the finishing machine for polishing the shoes on the other. My father was in the army during the First World War and his old tin hat hung up in the shop for years. In the room upstairs he kept racing pigeons – you had to deal in all sorts of things in those days. Sometimes he'd get a litter of dogs and they'd be in a tiny little room upstairs too! It must have been in 1940 when my father gave up the shoe shop and he never went back to shoe repairing."

"My uncle was a shoemaker too," John continues. "He was Frank Bunn, or 'Ditto' as he was known, and he lived next door to us in Vigilant Cottages where he used to work in his front room. Ditto's wife and my mother were sisters. Then there was another man who used to mend shoes by the name of Fred Lilley. He had no legs and used to go about on a little board with four wheels . . . We lived in four different places on the Beach, Vigilant Cottages, the *Rising Sun*, Jubilee Terrace and then just past Mrs Gibbs' later shop, in a little row of houses which are still there, at 287 Whapload Road. I can remember a Mrs Clark who was in that shop before Mrs Gibbs was, she used to sell a few sweets."

Another regular sight around the Beach in the 1930s was Walter Larke, who in the summer months used to drive around on a motor-bike with a side car, selling ice-cream. Walter also ran a billiard room, known as the Hiker's Rest, which was a youth club, situated in a building which had originally belonged to Wilde's School and had been known as the 'bottle room'. Alan Doy recalls, ". . . Walter Larke was married to my mother's sister, so he was my uncle. He lived in those cottages opposite the Alms Houses. In the Second World War Walter went into the Merchant Navy and got torpedoed. He survived and came out of the Navy and joined his family who had moved up to the Midlands. He died a short time later though, he never came back to the Beach."

"Cook's the butchers, they were on the Beach," remembers Ann Smith (née Wigg). "He used to bring his cattle down the Ravine and along Whapload Road, and there was always quite a do when they got to the place where they were going to be slaughtered. When they used to scoot, so did we!"

This is also recalled by Lydia Cullen (née Hammond). "Sometimes cows came along Whapload Road to Cook's the butchers shop, who had an abattoir at the side of their shop. The wall ran along the side of Maltsters Score and once, when several of the children stood there watching them coming along the road, one started to go wild and run away. It was a bit frightening but I think they could smell the abattoir. We all used to climb up on the wall and see the poor cows tied up for slaughtering."

There were several bakeries on the Beach Village, and one of the earliest of these was a place called the Hut or Noah's Ark Bakery, which stood on the west side of East Street where Ayers' net store would later be. In the 1920s there had been William Gray's bake-house, situated at 40 & 42 Whapload Road, while Arthur Maurice Binks had a bakery at 11 & 12 Rant Score East, which was taken over by

There were many bakeries on the Beach, and one of the earliest known of these was the Noah's Ark Bakery which was situated in East Street and shown here in the 1890s.

Eric Stanbridge in the mid 1930s. There was also Waller's Bakery at 60 Whapload Road, premises which had once been used as the North Beach Post Office. After the Second World War this became Bingham's, who already had another shop in Lowestoft, established in the early 1930s. "Bingham's Bakery had a window onto Whapload Road," recalls Michael Duncan, "which was painted up to a height which prevented pedestrians seeing in as they walked past. My friends and I would help each other to climb onto the window sill and gaze into the bakery where we could see the big ovens, the work bench and the baker pulling out the long trays containing pastries of all shapes and sizes from the ovens. On many occasions, he would pass to us all the off cuts from the cakes and sponges instead of throwing them away."

Before the Second World War, there was a refreshment stall on the sea wall, which was run by Mrs Violet Eva Collins. Mrs Collins was a member of the Cook family, who had business connections with the Grit in the days when the north beach was as popular as the South Beach and the Cooks opened chalets on the sea-wall for bathers. There were also cafes in the Beach Village. One was the *Corner Cafe* belonging to Mrs Bond, who was known as 'Blondie', which after the Second World War became Delf's shop. There was also the *Kumfy Kafe*, situated on the corner of Rant Score East and Anguish Street. It was run by Ron and Doris James in the early 1950s and Doris recalls, "We opened the *Kafe* in 1951. The place used to be a pub called the *Flowing Bowl* and we took it over. We had it as rooms and we turned the bar into a cafe. There were some people living in what had been the smokeroom and when they moved we took it over to open a fish shop, but the fish and chip shop was only open one night and then we all came down with the 'flu and before we had recovered we were flooded out in the '53 floods! We lost everything that night, and never opened again. All the tables and chairs were washed away and found near the Sparrow's Nest."

Despite the short time that the *Kumfy Kafe* was on the Beach, Mr and Mrs James were Beach people who knew the ways of the folk down there. Ron remembers, "When we were down there all the Scots girls and fishermen were still about, and Doris was dead crafty. She used to make hot coconut buns and work it so they came out of the oven at eleven o'clock, piping hot, and these big hairy-chested Scotsmen used to buy them by the dozen. You couldn't keep up with them!"

Opposite the *Rising Sun* public house was Harry Hammond's fish and chip shop, in premises which had once been another public house, *The Fishermen's Arms*. His daughter, Lydia Cullen, was born in 3 Jubilee Terrace but the family moved when her father bought the empty public house and converted it. She recalls, "It was a fairly large place. I expect many people from the Beach Village remember how we also used to sell shrimps, winkles, mussels and crabs, boiled in the copper at the back of the house. It was a very busy time in my young life, and many people would know my sister Lily, who used to serve in the fish shop. I am sure she must have been the fastest server in the Lowestoft area! The children used to call out to her and say, 'One penny of chips and a few scraps please'."

Lenny Norman was a regular at Hammond's, "I remember we used to get 'one and one', 1d of fish, 1d of chips, tuppence that would be. Sometimes if you were lucky he'd give you two fish, it all depended how he was, whether he had plenty of fish." Hammond's was also a favourite place for the Central School boys as Charles Ellis recalls, "Some of the boys would have fish and chip dinners and there'd be about thirty or forty boys dash round as soon as school finished and Lily used to

The photograph above shows a resident dressed for the Lowestoft carnival in the 1920s. Behind her can be seen the North Beach Post Office, which would later become Waller's and Bingham's bakeries. Situated on the corner of Whapload Road and Salter Street, this building (shown below after the Second World War), was bought by Birds Eye in the 1960s and used as their laundry.

A group of Watts Naval Boys outside Mrs Collins' tea stall on the sea wall. A bus service was also run along the sea wall at the time, and a bus can be seen on the horizon.

The Kumfy Kafe on its first day of opening in 1951. This was run by Ron and Doris James from what had once been the Flowing Bowl public house. The Kumfy Kafe closed after the 1953 flood.

say, 'Now, all behave yourselves, and you'll all get served!' There would be about thirty or forty fish and a bloody great stack of chips and it was good grub. It was all good wholesome food. You had a dab or a plaice, a good helping of chips, you had a good meal."

Past Hammond's, on the corner of Spurgeon Score was Wilson's Confectioners. Ronny Wilson recalls, "We lived in 4 East Street. My mother took up a business at the bottom of Spurgeon Score, a sweet business in a shop that used to be Cook's the butchers." In Anguish Street at No. 12 was Moss's sweet shop, a favourite with all the kids. Colin Dixon recalls, "Moss's sweet shop always had a cat in the window. Amongst the displays of sweets, there was always this cat. In those days we never bothered about it, but now I would think again." Ronny Wilson also remembers Moss's. "She had a little hole in her front window, and we used to put a little piece of wire through and pull the jelly-babies out"

"I was sometimes given a ha'penny on Saturdays," Eric Horne recalls from his 1930s childhood, "and would spend a long time in Gibbs' . . . deciding whether to buy two chocolate novelties at a farthing each or to spend the whole ha'penny on a marshmallow wafer."

Boothroyd's, Burwood's, Delf's, Squire's and Gibbs' are the best remembered grocery shops on the Beach but these establishments did not usually confine themselves to groceries, but would try to sell everything and anything that people wanted. Benjamin Burwood's shop was at 28 Whapload Road, near to the *Rising Sun* public house, and was listed in Kelly's Directory as a 'shopkeeper and confectioner'. However, as Ruby Timberley recalls, he sold a far wider variety of

An airship passing over the Beach Village in the 1930s. On the right can be seen Benjamin Burwood's grocery shop.

goods. "It was a little shop that sold almost every grocery, plus paraffin oil and candles. Since in the 1920s most houses had only oil lamps and candles as lighting they did quite well."

Michael Duncan's family bought their groceries from another of these Beach Village shops, "We obtained our groceries from Arthur 'Gibbies' shop and even after we moved to a new home he continued to deliver my mother's weekly order on a Friday night, in a car that made him seem a millionaire in our eyes."

The original Gibbs' shop was situated at 106–108 Whapload Road, opposite the Eagle Brewery. The shop opened in 1931 and was run by Nellie Gibbs and later by her son Arthur and his wife Iris. Iris recalls, "My late husband, Arthur, was born at Yarmouth in 1917 and he came to the Beach at fourteen when his mother, Nellie Annie, opened a little shop in the building which used to be the *Dutch Hoy* public house, where Birds Eye's offices are now. Arthur joined up at the outbreak of war but became a Japanese prisoner of war and didn't come home in 1945. We eventually married in 1949."

The shop was bombed during the Second World War and the Gibbs moved to 283 Whapload Road and have been there ever since. ". . . We lived there too," Iris continues, "but later we bought a cottage nearby for Arthur's Mum when she got too old to be on her own. We were here during the 1953 floods, didn't have time to save anything, and it was about three months before we could open again."

"When my husband died in January 1994 I decided to carry on. Arthur used to deliver groceries three nights a week, but I can't drive so when he died that had to stop. Since the houses were pulled down our customers have mostly been workmen, there are no locals these days. Now and again someone will pop in who I haven't seen for years and it's always nice to see old friends again. They're amazed I'm still here, but I am, open from seven to five every weekday!"

Mrs Iris Gibbs and her late husband Arthur, pictured in their shop at 283 Whapload Road which she still runs.

Iris Gibbs in the doorway of her shop in Whapload Road, 1997.

Boothroyds was on the corner of Herring Fishery Score where these had been a grocery shop since as far back as 1874 when John Gooderham was there. In the 1920s it was run by Mr Hatcher, though in the 1930s the shop was taken over by Willie Boothroyd, who was there for many years. The house next door was once known as the May Fly Inn which was kept by Abraham Porter in 1863. In 1865 William Alexander had acquired this property, describing himself as a 'beer retailer and hairdresser'.

On the corner of Wilde's Street, once known as Wilde's Score East, was at one time a bootmaker's shop. In later years it became Emery's grocery shop and was last occupied by Squire's, which is shown in the photograph.

After the Second World War Delf's grocery shop was established on the corner of Whapload Road and Hamilton Road in the premises formerly occupied by the Corner Cafe. Alan Delf, seen in the doorway of the shop, would sadly later take his own life.

Shops on the Beach circa 1925

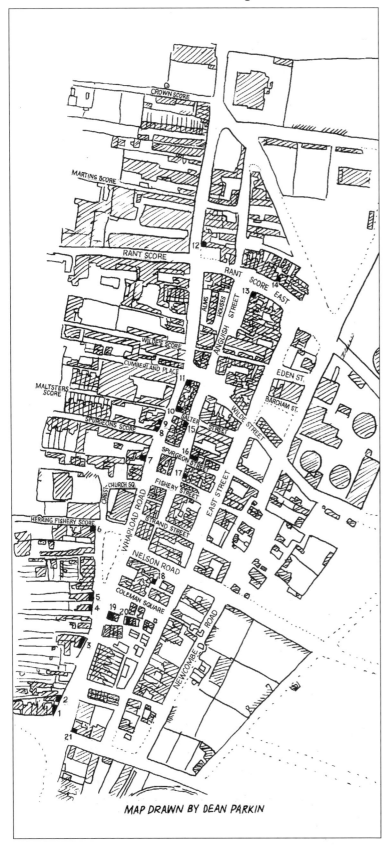

MAP DRAWN BY DEAN PARKIN

1. The Bishop sisters' shop was at 1 Whapload Road, and although the business was listed in the local directory as a confectioners it also sold other general grocery items, such as milk.

2. Their brother John Bishop had an ironmongery business at No. 3 Whapload Road, which later moved to London Road North. Another brother, Tom, then had the premises as a fishing tackle shop.

3. Pretty Son & Co. were decorators, situated at 25 Whapload Road. In 1934 Godfrey Girling the barber moved from 89 Whapload Road into these premises and remained there until 1940.

4. James T. Day was a basketmaker. Known locally as 'Jasper' he worked there but lived at 1 Nelson Road for many years.

5. Leslie Charles Peachman was selling bicycles from this site in 1925 but later had East Garage there.

6. In 1925 Cyril Provart was a grocer at 67 Whapload Road in a shop which had been used for this purpose for many years. In 1874 John Gooderham ran a similar establishment there, while Provart's predecessor was Mr H. G. Hatcher. In the 1930s the shop was taken over by Willie Boothroyd.

7. Hammond's fish and chip shop was situated near to Jubilee Terrace in a building which had formerly been the *Fishermen's Arms* public house.

8. Cook's the butchers could be found at 87 Whapload Road. By 1936 these premises were converted into a sweet shop which was run by Mrs Wilson, Ronny's mother.

9. Next door to Cook's was Joseph Flertey's dairy at 89 Whapload Road. In 1930 Godfrey Girling had his first barbers shop there.

10. 60 Whapload Road was vacant in 1925 but had previously been the North Beach Post Office. In the 1930s Waller's converted the building into a bakery and after the Second World War Bingham's could be found there.

11. Walter Emery had two grocery shops in the town in 1925, one in Mariner Street and the other on the Beach at 72 Whapload Road. In the 1930s this was taken over by Frederick Squire who ran the shop for the next thirty years.

12. Mrs Nellie Gibbs first opened a shop in the Beach Village in these premises at 106–108 Whapload Road, formerly the *Dutch Hoy* public house. Bombed during the Second World War, the Gibbs moved to 283 Whapload Road (off the map, northwards) and the shop remains open to this day.

13. In 1925 this property was the *Flowing Bowl* public house but in the 1930s it became Thurston's dairy. After the Second World War the building housed the *Kumfy Kafe* until the flood in 1953.

14. At 11 & 12 Rant Score East was Arthur Maurice Binks' Bakery which was taken over by Eric Stanbridge in the mid-1930s. This property was destroyed by bombing in the Second World War.

15. Wilson's fried fish shop was situated at 15–17 Anguish Street.

16. Many people remember Mrs Moss who had a sweet shop at 12 Anguish Street until the mid-1930s.

17. George Buck was a shoe repairer who had his shop at 8 Anguish Street for many years until he took over the *Rising Sun* in 1940.

18. Another baker, William Gray, had his premises at 40–42 Whapload Road.

19. Benjamin Burwood's general shop was next door to Canary Cottages at 28 Whapload Road.

20. Frank 'Ditto' Bunn was another shoe repairer on the Beach who worked from his front room at 1 Vigilant Cottages.

21. By the mid-1930s these premises were the *Corner Cafe*, run by Mrs Bond. After the Second World War Alan Delf had his shop here.

9

Fishing from the Beach

*". . . The Beach Village consisted of two lots of people;
those that went to sea in the drifters, and the rest of
them that worked in the kipper houses all over the village.
I suppose everybody relied on the drifters
and what they produced . . ."*

CHARLES ELLIS

"Most of my family worked on the Beach," recalls Harry Harper. "My grandad was originally a fisherman, but then came ashore and worked for Boardley's who carted the herring, my nanny worked for Dick Ayers in the fish house, my aunt Becky served in Flertey's shop on the Beach, and my aunt Nora worked in the steam laundry. My father and two uncles who lived with us, were all fishermen. My wife was a Scots fisher girl. I met her when she came down to Lowestoft in 1947 for the herring. She came down from Fraserburgh."

After the Second World War, the over-exploitation of the shoals resulted in dwindling catches and by the mid-1960s the home fishing voyage ceased altogether but at one time the arrival every autumn of the Scottish fleet and the fisher girls would have a huge impact on the Beach. The fishermen would purchase provisions and supplies from the shops and pubs, while the Scots girls and coopers would take board and lodgings on the Grit, benefitting many families and helping them to make ends meet. "Every September prior to the herring season," Ruby Timberley recalls, "the Scots girls would arrive at lodgings which had already been arranged for them by the firm they worked for. The men would go round the Beach Village seeking lodgings so that two or three could share. They needed to be as close as possible to the pickling plots, near to Hamilton Dock where the drifters landed the herring. The girls duly arrived with their large wooden boxes with all they would need whilst away from home. These came by lorry from their fishing boats."

"These 'girls' as we called them, though some were middle-aged, worked very hard in bitter weather, early and late. It was a great help to them to be able to earn their living and gave the people who took them into their homes a few pounds to help stock up with coal or buy their children some clothes for the winter. These Scots girls were a jolly lot. They didn't work on Sundays, but went to church or chapel. If during the week, owing to the weather, there was no fish for a couple of hours they were not idle but got out the jerseys they were knitting for their men folk."

"They would walk through the town in twos and threes, knitting and talking as they went. To us as children it sounded like a foreign language! We missed them when they left because some us would go to watch them working, their fingers wrapped round with rags to prevent the knives which they used so skilfully from cutting them. Some would gut herrings and some would pack the herring in barrels between layers of salt. The coopers put on the lids, knocked in wooden nails and then they were ready for export to Russia."

"We used to take in lodgers from Scotland, up to three at a time during the herring season," says Michael Duncan, "and conditions were fairly cramped then as we only had three bedrooms, and no bathroom. The fisher girls were very nice in their attitude and hard working, but my sister and I used to have great difficulty in understanding them. They used to go to work early after a breakfast of porridge sprinkled with salt and return home late afternoon ready for tea. I remember how they always had bandages on their fingers and how prominent the smell of fish was when they came home."

Lydia Cullen remembers, "My mother, Mrs Hammond, used to take in six girls. We had a large room at the side of our shop which, of course, was an old pub. My mum used to clear and clean the room. There was just an old fireplace and an electric light bulb and a cupboard where they stored some of their food as they cooked for themselves. A couple of days before they moved in the Scottish men would bring six great wooden trunks with their clothing and bed and blankets into this room and they were put around the room near the walls. This was their seating and also their beds. I think I was nine or ten years old when I used to take mugs of hot tea down to the pickling plots where the girls were working, gutting the herrings. I used to have to walk through Boardley's horse and cart shed. I think the old horses used to know me because when they saw me their heads used to lie hanging out of their sheds, thinking I would bring them food. It was a lovely time because the Scots were very friendly."

Mrs Rose Sansom (née Durrant) remembers, "The Scots girls would come down from the north of Scotland and work the herring fishing (when the silver darlings swam this way, in September to December). They would 'lay' toys in the shops (put money down to keep them) and when the settling up came at the end of the season, they would collect them, and take them down to their ship for the return journey back to Scotland. They did this with a barrel of grapes and a case of oranges and apples they purchased from my father, who was a wholesale fruit merchant in the town."

The Scots girls had a canteen hut built on the pickling plots where Eric Horne's mother had a job, cooking and cleaning. He can remember, "On Saturdays and at other times I helped out by collecting the dirty cups and became known by the girls as the 'Wee Bairn'. For lunch they ate Scotch broth which my mother prepared on a huge cooking range which had to be hot first thing in the morning. The eating area was kept warm by an old tortoise combustion stove. The girls also loved their jam doughnuts and iced buns which were delivered in great long trays from the local bakery."

"A perk of my mother's job was being given a large enamel jug of any left-over broth each day, together with a sheep's head, which had presumably flavoured the broth. Wrapped in newspaper the sheep's head was thrown over the high wall of a derelict building on the way home, but we all enjoyed the broth for our evening meal."

"Nurse Rae arrived with the Scots girls to keep them in check and to look after any injuries they suffered while gutting the herring. She was somewhat old but

A lorry load of Scots fisher girls, known by the locals as 'Scotch' girls.

Scots fisher girls gutting the herrings which have been sprinkled with salt and tipped into the 'farlins' (farlanes), the big wooden troughs they are shown standing over. Working in threes, the girls gutted and sorted the fish which were then packed head to tail in barrels, layered with salt. Every full barrel was covered and left for ten days then topped up with fish after the brine had been drained through the bung hole. The pickle was then replaced to ensure the fish were tightly packed.

The Scots girls on the pickling plots in the 1930s, with the gasworks in the background.

A fisher girl posing for a photograph on the pickling plots. "The Scots girls were very religious," remembers Charles Ellis. "One evening there was a lot of electrical activity out to sea and then suddenly, over the pickling plots, this huge cloud appeared which looked like Christ's head with a crown of thorns, and all this lightning behind it. It put the wind up all these Scots people, who thought it was the end of the world and they were all on the ground praying. Then the cloud broke up and it wasn't the end of the world and they all went home. This happened when I was young and it certainly frightened me!"

efficient and quite strict. She was always the last to leave the hut in the evening and on the way up Rant Score to her digs, she would pop the keys through our letter-box for my mother to open up next morning. One morning my mother arrived to find the hut broken into – goodness knows what they hoped to find!"

Leonard Boyce lived with his grandparents at the *East of England* public house on Whapload Road. He remembers, "When the fisher girls were doing the gutting they used these old acetylene lamps or flares, and of course the smoke used to pour off these things and the whole area was full of smoke. But how those women worked in the weather they did; the snow even, they'd still be gutting herrings! These horse drawn carts used to come with loads of fish which were tipped in the troughs and fast as they could gut them so they'd fill them up, it was remarkable."

"My grandmother took four of them in, these Scots fisher girls, staying with us at the pub. I think she gave them one bedroom and I had to move into my aunt's room, we only had three bedrooms I believe. They always used to have bandages on every finger to protect themselves instead of gloves. When they used to come in from the other side of the road where they'd been gutting they had great heavy boots on, oil skins down to their ankles, perhaps a scarf round the head. They used to come in, and they'd stand out in the yard and take all their gear off. Of course they couldn't come indoors like that, stinking of fish, herring all over their boots, but no matter

The original pickling plots were opposite the East of England, and the pub can be seen here in the background, behind the barrels, left of centre. "The pub was quite busy in the 1920s," remembers Leonard Boyce whose grandfather was landlord, "especially during the fishing time, because we had all the Scots down here."

LOWESTOFT. THE PICKLING PLOTS. 207

*Before the mid-1920s the pickling plots were situated to the north of the Beach Village, opposite the
Crown Score area. Subsequently they moved to the more familiar Hamilton Road site, pictured below.*

how cold it was or how wet it was, they'd take everything off outside and put it in the shed, and then they'd come in and go straight through to their room. We had the same four girls for about three years, they came about October and went home just before Christmas."

"I can also remember how they used to load up the 'Klondikes' as they were called, or the ships from Russia which used to come in to pick up the barrels of herring. The horses and carts used to stand on the road for hours and hours waiting to go on the fish market to load the fish, queued up from the old trawl market, Waveney Road, right round as far as Battery Green, queuing to load up the ships. Hours they used to stand! The horses used to stand there and sleep and the drivers did and all, I reckon!"

Many of the children from the Beach Village would visit the curing yards to try to scrounge a few herring and, though the yard foreman sometimes chased them away, one way of getting free fish was to cheek the Scots girls who would then throw one or two herrings at them. The girls would be told off for doing this but they retaliated with a few well-chosen words and the foreman would usually beat a hasty retreat. What he didn't know was that as the Scots girls threw the herring at the children, they would give them a wink, knowing that they would be taking them home to tea!

Sometimes though fish would simply just be given to you. Mrs Myrtle Porter (née Durrant) remembers, "I can remember that when I was a girl, all the fisher girls used to gut the fish and pack the barrels outside the front of our house in Newcombe Road. We faced the pickling plots and we used to go and watch them and they used to give us bucket loads of fish. We had a lot of fish!"

In October 1936 the Scots girls went on strike over their pay, demanding an extra two pence a barrel, and two shillings and sixpence extra lodging allowance. Meetings were held on Battery Green, which in those days was a stretch of grassland, and it was here that tempers rose and some colourful language was spoken as the girls fought for their rights.

During this strike, some of the girls carried on working and had to be protected by the police, as words flew along with one or two gutting knives. The strike ended when the drifters were brought almost to a standstill and the Herring Board were forced to relent, although the girls never got the lodging allowance they asked for.

By this time the Scottish fleet had considerably reduced in size, and the following year herring catches on the home voyage were just a third of the 1913 level. Most of the European markets for herring had collapsed and the silver shoals had become rarer and unpredictable, all resulting in hardship for the fisherman between the wars. Money had always been scarce in fishing families. Even in the decade before the First World War when the herring industry was at its height, it wasn't the fishermen who made the profit, but the skippers and the boat owners.

"Dad was a chief engineer on the drifters," recalls Bert Prettyman, "and after the home fishing season he would have to go on the beach and pick stones. I can remember taking a flask of tea down to him. When you think, he was a chief engineer with all the papers to prove it, and these time-served men had to go on the beach and pick up stones. It must have been very degrading but it was all to give us something to eat."

"At the age of thirteen my Dad stowed away on a trawler," Yvonne Scriggins adds, "which gave him the taste for the sea. After that he became a fisherman sailing the fishing smacks and trawlers . . . In the 1920s work was very depressed so if there

When the fishing was bad fishermen would sometimes resort to picking up stones on the north beach, for which they were paid by the bucket-load. The flints they collected were then split by stone breakers and used for making roads.

was no fishing he had to look elsewhere . . . . He would perhaps hear of a job but that would mean standing in line with many more men, so he could be queuing from approximately two o'clock in the morning to stand a chance of the job. Many a time he would comb the beach for coal or wood washed ashore, with a wife and eight children they needed any work that brought in money . . . While combing the beach one day (during the war) he came across an unexploded bomb. Having notified the authorities, they offered him work filling sandbags and then repairing the sea wall . . . He did other jobs such as washing down the floor of the fish market; by doing this there was always a chance he would get free fish. He sold papers and if he sold twelve he would be paid threepence. When he was fishing he would be away for weeks fishing in the North Sea, Aberdeen, North Shields or wherever the fish were. Dad's life was a struggle."

Many times fishermen could be away for a week or ten days and when they returned to shore have nothing to show for the journey. With the long periods away fishing, or just chasing work around the country, family life was difficult for these men. John Day's father was one such fisherman. "His name was Bobbie Day, a small balding man who had a taste for rum when coming off fishing trips. But off-season he would travel round Britain trying to get a job, on any ship, as a cook. He died at 35 and the sad thing was, because he was never really in my young life, I didn't notice his passing. He simply did not return from a fishing trip."

Norma Wilson's father was Vernil Tuck, who was a lifeboatman for many years. She recalls, "Because my Dad was a fisherman he used to go away for quite a while and when he came home my eldest sister used to cry because she didn't know who he was. Then my Mum said,' I'm not putting up with this,' so that's why he gave up the sea, to get a job on the land."

Michael Duncan lived in Wilde's Street next to the *Gas House Tavern*. He recalls, "My father was a fisherman in drifters and spent many years spent on the *Adel* and the *Tritona* and like many other doing the same job was away from home for much of my childhood. On his rare occasions at home I can remember being taken for walks along the Denes towards Sparrow's Nest, trying my best to jump up to and swing off the goalposts they used to hang the nets from. I can remember holding his hand which was big and strong but above all, the skin was dry, taut and so hard, caused by sheer hard work."

Fishing or a related job was in many cases all the Beach Village had to offer. The only way of bettering your lot was to become a skipper, as fishermen tended to leave the Beach Village when they became skippers. Despite this, some boys wanted to go to sea. Leonard Boyce was one such boy, his grandfather, Lenny Tripp, having been a fisherman. Leonard recalls, "I crazed him to go out on one of these boats, the *Christmas Daisy* it was called. 'All right, boy,' he said, 'they're going out to test the compass, you can go out for a few hours.' So we went out near the Claremont Pier and I was sick as a toad. I think I was in bed two days after, I was really bad I was. The cook kept coming and asking if I wanted tea and all sorts of things, and it really stunk, with that smell of oil and whatever, and of course they were rolling the boat about to test this compass on the top of the wheelhouse. Anyway, I had enough of that and I never went to sea any more in all my life, I've never been on the water since."

The hard life of fishing offered little in the way of security and the risks of this thankless job were all too regularly illustrated. "In 1930 when I was just two years old, my father was lost at sea," recalls Eric Horne, "He was on a fishing vessel working the cod ground. Although a cooper by trade, he was no stranger to the sea having served in the Navy in the Great War, and if work was scarce it had to be taken where it could be found. My mother was left a widow with three young boys to raise on her own. I was the youngest, Ernest was five, and Fred was nine."

"The widows' pension, (known, I recall, as the Lloyd George pension) of just ten shillings a week, did not go very far. Whatever work came along had to be taken. Charring (housework for the better off) brought in two shillings a day, while other jobs included making or repairing fishing nets and peeling onions for pickling at a house down Old Nelson Street. For this job we all gave a hand at home, washing hundred of salvaged jam jars which my brothers and I then delivered to the pickling house in a barrow made from a sugar box and old pram wheels. From the pension of ten shillings a week, my mother had to pay 4/6d rent for our four-roomed terraced cottage at 4 Rant Score, which was owned by a Mr Beamish."

Yvonne Scriggins' mother Hilda May Gurney, who died in July 1983, also had a family heavily involved with the fishing industry. "She was born in Lowestoft in 1910 . . . Hilda had two brothers Ernest and Jack, also a sister Clara . . . Jack, the youngest, was on board a fishing smack when it was run down by a liner. No-one survived and Jack was only 17 or 18 years old when he drowned . . . My mother's father William John Gurney, also had a bad accident at sea and lost an eye plus other injuries. Sadly, he died at the age of 45 years. Nan ran a fish shop on the Beach, but Nan being Nan would never be rich as she was always nipping into the *Gas House Tavern* for a drink!"

"Many men lost their lives at sea," Yvonne continues. "While he was on the trawlers my Dad did all the cooking and he always could cook a good meal but he had a very bad accident at sea which resulted in him losing a finger, plus badly damaging his arm which prevented him from working for quite a while. Compensation took a long time coming through and involved his being checked by different doctors. He received £200 which at that time was good . . . On the occasions when the fishing catch was good they were paid out in sovereigns. Whenever he got paid, he and the rest of the crew would head for the nearest pub although, having said that, he always made sure his family had food on the table, and clothes . . . Even when Dad was old, the sea was still in his blood and he often talked about the boats he sailed in, *Peaceful, Bonny Lass, Antelope* and the *Consolidated*."

*   *   *   *

A steam drifter and a sailing trawler, known as a 'smack', leaving the harbour for the fishing grounds in 1910.

The Hosanna, a typical example of a steam drifter.

There was great competition to reach the fishing grounds first, and here we can see the drifters racing away from port.

Herring being unloaded from the boat by fishermen using quarter-cran baskets, one cran equalling 1320 fish.

A scene at the Fish Market, showing the fishermen discharging their catch into cases for export to Germany.

In 1950 the metal boxes replaced the wooden ones. Easier to clean, the metal boxes were also taken to sea and sometimes, if the fishermen didn't have enough fish to return to port, they would pack the fish into the boxes and stay out another night.

Local girls working for Sayer and Holloway in 1920.
Back row, left to right, Violet Clark, Violet Keith, Jessie Hitter (née Harper), Connie Hugman,
Emma Pickess, Mrs Hemsby, Lily Harper.
Front row, Gladys Falkner, Annie Johnson, Bessie Bowler, Clara Gurney, Eve Osborne,
Emma Sturman.

10

A Home for Industry

*"Really, you have to be pleased with the
industrial estate that's down there now because
of all the labour that it brings to the town."*

HAZEL BOARDLEY

The Beach Village has always been an industrial area, although at one time most of
the industries to be found there were related to fishing. "There were a lot of beating
chambers where many young girls were employed mending nets," Lydia Cullen
recalls. "There was always a smell of tanning and when they were finished they were
hung over poles on the Denes and there are still some poles standing there. It was
a quite exciting time because it was very busy and full of activity. My sister Stella
was a good one for mending nets."

Herring nets were made at Beeton's Sunrise Net Works in East Street and tanned
for strength in the net yards while the net stores housed the fishing gear between
trips. An essential part of each store was the beating chambers where the nets were
repaired by a team of beatsters. Before the nets were tanned or 'barked' in the tan
copper, they would be checked by ransackers, and it was this whole process that
provided many jobs for the people of the Beach Village.

At the start of the twentieth century, a beatster's wage was eight or nine shillings
a week, although apprentices received nothing for the first year and only two and
sixpence a week during their second year. Due to the large amount of nets that
needed to be mended, many were repaired at home as well as on the chambers.
Women would work in the evening by oil lamp and in every house where a beatster
lived you could find a beatster's hook, which was a big staple driven into the woodwork around the window or into the door-frame for this purpose. During the 1920s
and '30s women working on the trawl nets was common practice. "I remember an
aunt of mine did this work," says Ruby Timberley. "The owner sent the bales of
twine by horse and cart to houses. My sister and I filled spools for our aunt, so that
she could carry on working away at her net without stopping. She started by casting
on with a loop on a hook above the sitting room door. These nets became very
heavy and the horse and cart would collect the finished nets."

Gowing's Ropeworks operated in this area for over a century. Their ropewalk was
established in 1790 and was a quarter of a mile long, running parallel to the north
end of Whapload Road. The ropery buildings could be found facing the 'hanging
gardens' of the High Street, and consisted of a winding room, dressing chambers,
tar-house, rope store and offices. At one time in this area there was also a twine
ground, where men would spin the big ropes which were used for trawl warps, tow

Beeton's Sunrise Net Works in East Street.

Photograph taken in October 1947 showing beatsters at work in the Shoals, a net store situated at the bottom of Lighthouse Score.
From left to right, Rita Sharman, Flo Balls, Cissy Freestone, Vina Harris, Ernie Woolner, Edna Fiske, Gerty Woolner, Doris Willgoss, Pauline Harris and Kitty Waller.

ropes and cables. Towards the end of the nineteenth century Gowing closed, due to a slump in fishing, the arrival of wire ropes, and the effect of the big roperies at Gourock, Belfast and Edinburgh. Gowing's property was bought in 1887 by the Lord of the Manor, Mr R. H. Reeve, and was then acquired with the rest of the Denes by the council when Reeve died four years later. The ropery buildings were then demolished, but the walk remains to this day as a roadway between the posts and nets on which Lowestoft fishermen still have the right to dry their nets. Other minor ropemakers in the Beach Village were S. S. Francis and Mr S. Saunders who both had premises in Whapload Road.

Boat building was also prevalent on the Beach. In 1785 Thomas Johnson obtained a permit from the Lord of the Manor to build a shed on the waste or beach, 'abutting on the Whapload Way'. The small plot of land rented was 40 ft. x 20 ft. and was on the corner of Whapload Way and Rant Score East where a shed was built, probably for stores, and a saw-pit. There was also Barcham's yard some-where in the same area, Barcham being the builder of the *Frances Ann* lifeboat in 1807 which is recorded as having cost £200. The exact site of the yard is unknown, but in May 1838 the Lowestoft Paving committee inspected the end of the town drain 'on the beach near Mr Barcham's boatbuilding yard', and 'recommended that such drain be lengthened the full width of the intended road . . .' So wherever the drain and the intended road met nearby was Barcham's yard.

One short-lived and ill-fated venture that has almost slipped from memory was the salt factory, which was built near Ness Point in the late 1920s. Lenny Norman recalls, "They started to build a salt factory. They were going to refine the salt from the sea but that never worked for them. That was on the pickling plots in the 1920s and stood there empty for years and years . . . When the Scots girls used to come here, they built themselves a little hut where they used to go and have their tea, and this was alongside the salt factory."

Charles Ellis can also remember this. "The salt factory was just to the right of Ness Point, as near to the sea as they could get. It was there in the late 1920s. I lived in Scarle's Buildings and as you walked up the road, it was dead opposite, near Ness Point itself. There was a high wall around the factory, which had a great big chimney. Inside there were these huge trays made of steel and underneath were furnaces. Those huge trays were where they put the salt water which was pumped straight from Ness Point. The water was heated to get the salt out. The idea was that they could use it for the curing of herring but something went wrong, they never thought it out. What they didn't realise was that when they pumped in all this water, there would also be a certain amount of sand amongst it so they were getting sand in their salt, and there was no way they could separate it. So whoever built that factory must have lost a lot of money."

Richard Ayers' Fish Merchants and Curers had premises near to the Steam Laundry on the east side of Whapload Road. Established in 1870 by George Thomas Ayers, the company later added some stables, which they converted into garages when motor vehicles replaced horses. At the beginning of the twentieth century the firm was known as Ayers Brothers Ltd, but by the early 1920s had become Richard Ayers Ltd, and although the building received damage from a bomb blast during the Second World War, the company continued until 1953. These premises were subsequently taken over by the Belfast Ropework Company, until 1968 when they were sold to Birds Eye Foods who had them demolished in March 1969, and built their offices there.

Arthur Gouldby was a fish merchant who had premises abutting on to Scarle's Buildings. This picture shows Gouldby's refrigerated lorry fleet, a rarity in those days, lined up off Whapload Road in the 1950s. This is now the site of the Birds Eye canteen.

The firm of Clifford Arthur Gouldby was another company of fish merchants and curers to be found on the Beach. Gouldby's had premises on the west side of Whapload Road, abutting on to Scarle's Buildings, and had a fleet of lorries delivering boxes of freshly-landed Lowestoft fish to customers over a wide area. The Gouldby family had been long associated with buying and selling fish in Lowestoft, and by the 1950s the fleet comprised of refrigerated lorries, which were something of a rarity in those days.

Some of the most familiar lorries, and before that carts, on the Beach were those belonging to the Boardleys. Billy Keith remembers, "They used to run up and down Whapload Road to the the fish market, and take all the fish in carts up to the north quay to be lowered into the boats and taken away. And there'd be carts all along Commercial Road, waiting, and they were just going round in a continuous circle, back and forth all these horses and carts. Boardley's also used to supply the horses for the rocket teams . . ."

The Boardley Brothers were established in the second half of the nineteenth century but by the end of that century had split into two separate businesses, both hauling contractors. "They started off as the Boardley Brothers," Matthew Boardley explains. "This was my grandfather and his brothers, but then they had a difference of opinion and they broke apart into two businesses. There was A. & S. Boardley and M. Boardley, who was my grandfather. They had premises nearly next door to each other, both off East Street. They both did the same work and were in competition with each other. My father took over from his father, and when he died

Matthew Boardley, pictured above, taking the reins of one of his carts, with his son Matthew by his side.

Matthew Boardley took over M. Boardley's haulage company from his father who had established the business when the original Boardley Brothers company split up at the end of the nineteenth century. When he died in 1943 this branch of the business finished as his son, also called Matthew, says, ". . . I was at Coventry then, before I left to serve in India, but my mother didn't want me to take on the business . . ."

Ronnie Boardley with some of his lorries at the rear of his haulage business in the Beach Village. Before the Second World War, when Arthur and Sam Boardley ran this company, horse and carts had been used for this haulage work.

in 1943, the business on our side of the family all finished. I was at Coventry then, before I left to serve in India, but my mother didn't want me to take on the business."

The premises of A. & S. Boardley were in Nelson Road, just off East Street, and were founded by Arthur and Sam Boardley who began trading with horse drawn vehicles in the mid-1890s, their work mainly being carting herrings. In the 1920s lorries were added to their fleet of vehicles and eventually the business was taken over by Samuel's son Ronnie. By this time the vehicle fleet was completely mechanised and they continued operations until 1968.

Conrad Smith's grandfather was a haulage contractor who was taken over by Boardley's. "His name was Edward 'Lump' Ellis," Conrad remembers. "When he was delivering the Klondike boxes opposite Birds Eye he would sometimes stop for a little drink, but it was all right because if he had too much they would lay him on the cart and the horse would take him home! My mother's uncle was Jack Gooderham. He was a coal merchant and had a place at the bottom of Rant Score."

The three gas holders which once dominated the skyline were part of the gas-works. The town's first gasworks were built in 1837 by a Mr James Malam and cost £2,500 to build, including a gas holder with a capacity of 8,000 cubic feet. This began as only a modest enterprise, with the whole gas holder holding only £2 worth of gas, and it was from here that the gas was supplied for the first lamps in Lowestoft's streets. In 1852 a new company was formed who bought the gasworks for £8,000, with the objective of supplying gas for the lighting of the town on a more permanent basis. A major expansion got under way and the service was improved, and in 1864 the first gas main was put down across the harbour to take supplies to the south of the town. For nearly a century Lowestoft continued to make its own gas supply, until 1963 when the town began to take gas from the 'grid' until coal gas gave way to natural gas from the North Sea. In 1964 the old hundred-foot chimney at the works was demolished and in 1975 the two older gas holders which had served the town since 1882 and 1904 respectively, were pulled down, leaving just the newer one, built in 1965 with a capacity of a million cubic feet, remaining.

Ness Point Works, situated on the corner of Maltsters Score, was the home of Rist's Wires and Cables. Leonard Boyce worked for them before the Second World War and says, "When I left school I had a couple of herring boy jobs, and then I got a job at Rist's where I met my wife and we married in 1939. I was there when war broke out when I was 23 and I had a reserved occupation at first. They were doing government work, cables for aircraft and things and so they were evacuated because of the invasion scare. They moved to Nuneaton and we went with them, in June 1940, and worked there until I was called up in 1942. Then I found out I that I had an ear problem that kept me on home service in England which was lucky for me really because I might not have been here now. Pals that I trained with who went to Italy all got killed."

On the corner of Rant Score was Youngman and Preston's Eagle Brewery. Established around 1856 as Youngman and Son, it was not until around 1870 that Preston became a partner. In 1919 the company was absorbed by Lacons of Great Yarmouth and the Eagle brewery was sold to Charrington and Co. Ltd. After the Second World War it was acquired by Birds Eye, and was demolished in September 1958, to make way for new developments. One of the two stone eagles, once the symbol of Youngman and Preston's, was broken whilst being removed, but the other was saved and is displayed over the entrance to the Birds Eye cafeteria on Whapload

Gooderham's coal cart leaving the south end of Whapload Road. On the left can be seen the two shops belonging to the Bishop family.

Inside the Lowestoft gasworks in the 1930s.

An early motorized delivery vehicle belonging to the Youngman and Preston Company, who had their offices at 69 High Street and Grosvenor House in Lowestoft.

The yard of the Eagle Brewery which was situated on the north side of Rant Score. This was owned by Youngman and Preston and was closed after the 1914–18 War.

Road. By this time Birds Eye had began to grow across the site of the Beach Village, and had surrounded the building of the Steam Laundry, which is still running to this day and is another old business from the Grit. The laundry premises were built in the late 1880s opposite Crown Score and there was a great deal of opposition over the construction from local boat-owners, who insisted that the land was part of their net drying grounds and there should be no enclosures on the Denes. Birds Eye, who now surround the old Steam Laundry building with their high-tech factories, have also met opposition in the past over building on the Denes. Their immense plant has grown and developed over the site of the old Beach Village and has become a big investment for the company who are now the biggest employer in the town.

Birds Eye Walls, as they are now known, came to Lowestoft in 1949, opening a small depot which soon grew to a complete production unit by 1952. That was the same year that the company invested £70,000 which provided the plant required for freezing peas and in the subsequent decades the Birds Eye factory along Whapload Road has grown and gone from strength to strength. To meet increasing demands the massive Steakhouse building was built in the mid-1980s, and in 1988 the company's entire vegetable repack operation was transferred here, in addition to a third potato line the following year. The development of the factory has continued into the 1990s, and following a £18,000,000 investment, Denes IV was opened in 1993, with three lines running continuously twenty-four hours day and seven days a week. The factory now has five main production buildings over an area of some thirty-one acres and has around 1,500 employees.

Although it seems a shame that these modern industrial buildings have covered any trace of the Beach Village, it has to be remembered that the Beach has always been an industrial site of sorts, providing jobs for the surrounding community. Where once, at the beginning of the twentieth century, over 2,500 lived and worked on this site in what now seems primitive and poor conditions, at the end of the same century a number nearing that figure still work on the very same ground with a higher standard of living.

The Lowestoft Steam Laundry building on Whapload Road. This was erected in the late 1880s and met with a great deal of controversy over the legality of building on such a site. It seems that the laundry was built across a public roadway in defiance of the Town Council who had refused to sanction the plans. However, the building stayed and is now surrounded by the complex of Birds Eye factories.

In the 1950s Birds Eye began to expand across the Beach Village, utilising many of the existing properties, and by 1960 the company were employing 1400 at peak periods. Here we see how they built on the front of Wilde's Cottage, which was used as their first personnel office.

Contemporary photograph looking north down Whapload Road showing Christ Church and the surrounding industrial estate built on the site of the Beach Village.

Mr Alfred Breach working at Beeton's Sunrise Networks in East Street. Although beatsters were usually women, men did do the work, and were paid more to do the same job.

11

The Thirsty Breed

*"All those pubs down there got a living because
there were such a lot of people on the Beach."*

LENNY 'WINKY' NORMAN

In 1900, in the days when the price of beer varied from 1d to 1½d a pint, there were thirteen pubs and beer-houses in the Beach Village. Fishermen were a thirsty breed and at a time when the population of the Beach Village itself was over two thousand five hundred, their number swelled every autumn by the influx of fishermen for the herring season, there were more than adequate numbers to fill these public houses.

The smaller beer houses were actually no more than front rooms. These came about because in the middle of the last century anyone assessed for poor rate was entitled to a licence to sell beer. The cost of the licence was £2. 2. 0d a year and the result was a boom in beer houses. 'Much evil resulted' says a report on these times and finally in 1860 the Justices Licence was introduced.

Drink was a problem in some cases, and to try to combat its allure the Church of England Temperance Society opened five coffee houses in Lowestoft in 1879, two of which, the *Lifeboat Tavern* and the *Tea Pot*, were situated in Whapload Road. The *Lifeboat Tavern* was on the south side of Whapload Road, to the south of Christ Church and was actually a residence which had been turned into a temperance house. In one of its bay windows there was a sign which said, "A public-house without the drink, where men can sit, talk, read and think. And sober home return."

Drinking was very much part of the fisherman's life though. Lenny Norman's late brother, Bob 'Umshi' Norman told a local newspaper in September 1966, "Every drifter started the season with beer. The crew used to have two gallons of beer and bread and cheese for fitting out and I used to take it down to the boats with a nanny goat and cart. Then there was hot stout to be taken over day and night to the women working in the smoke houses."

The Norman family pub was the *Suffolk Fishery Tavern* which was situated in Anguish Street. Lenny Norman was born above the pub in 1921 by which time his parents had been running the tavern for about four years although his father had originally been a fisherman and his mother a braider. Lenny recalls, "They used to open at five o'clock in the morning in the fishing time for the drivers of the carts and for rum and beverages up to breakfast for the herring workers. At that time my mother used to take some Scots people in, coopers, and they came down from Wick, employed by the McCormacks and she was paid at the end of the season, when they went home. The money then was five shillings a head allowance to feed them on, and there used to be about six of them in there including the main cooper at the time . . . In the pub we had a 'snug'. The women used to come in there, sometimes early in the morning, when all their husbands had gone to work. Come in with a jug and fill it up with beer to take home."

When Lenny was six, his family gave up the pub due to his mother's ill health, "So we had to move," he explains. "We'd had the pub about ten years when Walter Strange took it over. He became landlord until it came to close, but as far as I can remember that didn't stay open long after we left." Indeed, in 1927 the pub was de-licensed and closed.

The names of the Beach Village pubs came from many sources, with the *Dutch Hoy* and *Fishermen's Arms*, derived from the fishing industry, and the *Princess Royal* named after an Old Company yawl. The *Inkerman Arms* and the *Balaclava* commemorated British battles which had been fought abroad while the *East of England* and the *Rising Sun*, referred to the locality of the area, the latter also becoming known as the Japanese Embassy!

The *Princess Royal* was situated on the corner of Nelson Road and East Street and was run for many years by Mr Wilfred George Jones, who was landlord when the premises were modernised in the late 1920s. The pub had been in this family for ninety years when they left in the early 1930s, to take on a newly built pub, the *Norman Warrior* in Oulton Road in the town. Wilfred died on February 14th 1933, aged 56 years, leaving a wife, two daughters and a son, Billy, who were all well known locally. The younger daughter, Ada, born on 30th December 1916, can still remember the old pub on the Beach. She recalls, "Our living quarters were in an adjoining building but years ago there was a club room above the pub where the old fishermen used to sit and talk."

In the early 1900s the *Princess Royal* was the home of one of the town's best fund raisers for the Royal National Lifeboat Institution. This was Spot the dog who had been trained by Wilfred Jones to do various begging tricks and for these he was given money which was deposited in the lifeboat collecting box. In 1908 it seems this little fox-terrier collected more money than was contained in all the other lifeboat collecting boxes in the town added together! As a result the Institution presented the dog with a silver collar suitably inscribed. Spot's death in 1910 was reported in a local newspaper, which stated, ". . . The honourable secretary told the annual meeting of the Royal National Lifeboat Institution about the death of our canine friend at the *Princess Royal*. This dog has provided a considerable sum to the Institution through collection boxes. Although Mr Jones is training another dog to replace our late friend, it will be some time before it is as accomplished as the other helper." The dog was given a fitting burial, ". . . enclosed in a handsome coffin with brass fittings . . ."

Leonard Boyce lived with his grandparents who ran the *East of England* public house which was situated on Whapload Road. "I wasn't born on the Beach, I was born in Tennyson Road. My father was killed in the First World War and my mother remarried, in 1922 I think it was. I was about six years old and my step-father was one who didn't want step-children and so my grandparents took me and brought me up and that's how I came to get on the Beach. It was about 1923–24 I went down there and I was brought up in a pub called the *East of England*, which was the last pub before you got to the Sparrow's Nest. My grandfather was Leonard Tripp, a boat owner who made a bit of money from fishing during the First World War then he took this pub, moving from Old Nelson Street, and I went with them."

"I was never allowed in the pub. If I stuck my head round the door, it would be,

The Princess Royal was on the corner of Nelson Road and East Street. Here we see the pub before it was modernised in the late 1920s, with the landlord, Wilfred Jones, pictured second from left. Also in the picture is Spot, who was one of the town's best fund-raisers for the Royal National Lifeboat Institution.

The Princess Royal after modernisation. The Jones family had run this pub for ninety years when they left in the early 1930s, and the pub subsequently closed.

Leonard Tripp, licensee of the East of England public house. The first reference to this pub can be found in 1879 when it was run by Edward Field. After 1934 it ceased to be a tavern and became the headquarters of the Ness Point Angling Club, with Leonard Tripp as secretary. "The old man was manager of that till he died in 1941," remembers Leonard Boyce.

'Boy! Out of there!' that was my grandfather. He was very strict in some ways but a nice old boy really. My dear old grandmother was stone deaf from birth, she never heard anything. I did used to have a nose in the bar to see what was going on at times, especially if he wasn't there, and I remember the beer was drawn out of a wooden tap, not pumps or anything like that. They were busy though, and it was surprising in the summer how many visitors would stroll down there and come and sit in the backyard, where we had round tables."

"At the back of the *East of England* was a long garden, a terrifically long garden, and there used to be a couple of brothers, called Miles, who made twine in this yard, I think they paid my grandfather rent for using the yard. They used to wrap it round their waists and go backwards right from the top of the yard to the bottom, making this twine, and some youngster sat at the top turning a wheel, and I used to help out with that sometimes. I got sixpence or a shilling a week if I helped them."

"Our sitting-room was behind the bar, with just this glass partition separating it. I could see through the frosted glass though, what was going on. The pub itself was like a lot of those pubs down Whapload Road, you wouldn't call them pubs today. There was one long bar and a small smoke-room at the back. They would throw sawdust down on the wooden floor and there were a couple of spittoons there too. The Miles brothers, who used to do the twine spinning, as soon as they finished, their first call was the pub and one of them acted as bouncer, he used to get his beer free I think. He stood up the corner and he was ever such a big fella, and if there was any trouble he'd throw them out."

"The pub was quite busy in the 1920s, especially during the fishing time, because we had all the Scots down here using the pub. Very often they'd have fights in the road, especially on Saturday nights. The Scots lads would come in, mix with our lot, and get drunk and finish up outside, eleven o'clock at night, and I used to peek through the window and see this lot fighting, and down would come the police, on their bicycles in them days, two or three of them trying to sort 'em out."

"I can remember my grandfather fighting sometimes, he used to get in these brawls. It didn't happen every week but I can remember it happening. There'd be an argument and they'd get outside fighting. I remember one night he got mixed up in this and he came in with the knee out of his trousers, blood on the side of his face, and he was a-swearing. Of course, his poor old lady would get worried and upset sitting in the back sitting room, knowing what was going on. She used to go upstairs to the bedroom and look out of the front bedroom window to see what was going on. I would be in there with her and tell her all about the noise."

Like any pub, the *East of England* had its regulars, men who spent many a long hour in an atmosphere thick with smoke from pipes and cigarettes, telling yarns over a pint. Leonard continues, "Some of them old chaps who used to come in that pub had their names engraved on the seats, had little bits of wood with their names on! About half a dozen of 'em like that. And very often they'd come in that pub dinner-time on a Saturday and wouldn't go out until about ten or eleven at night. They never went home to dinner, just sat there drinking or playing cards."

"One regular character that sticks in my mind is 'Happy' Welham, him and his donkey. He was a peculiar looking man, great big nose and sort of hunched up. He used to live in Lighthouse Score and he'd come out of there, along Whapload Road with his donkey and cart and little dog, get as far as the *East of England* and stop. Into the pub he'd come, and sit there for a time, and I can't ever remember seeing him over-drinking, but he was always very happy as they called him!"

"I remember my grandfather used to have this big slate where he put the fishermen's debts down, especially the Scotsmen. They used to come in there and drink all the voyage, when they were in from sea, and always put it on the slate and they always used to pay up before they went home near Christmas. I don't ever remember him complaining that any of them had let him down."

"Things went all wrong in the 1930s, but he kept on there till he died. During that period he had a big net store on the east side of Whapload Road. Nearly opposite the pub there was a big net chamber run by a firm called Westgate, and a little further along was my grandfather's, it was isolated, it stood all alone on the Denes. It was a big place with two storeys. It had a tanning copper for the nets, and I can remember the women going up there mending the nets, sorting out the new nets ready to go to sea. A whole row of them would stand mending the nets. I used to have a rare old time running about the net chamber."

"I remember many of the old pubs down there although I was too young to go into them. The brewers for the *East of England* were Morse's who were in Crown Street, and that's where he used to get his beer from. I think Morse's owned the pub and when they finished, the pub finished but somehow it was kept open as the Denes Fishing Industry Club and we just carried on and the old man was manager of that till he died in 1941."

Perhaps two of the most remembered of the Beach Village pubs were the *Gas House Tavern*, and the *Rising Sun*. Alice Coleman, formerly Mrs Brady, kept the *Gas House Tavern* for about four years from the late 1940s. "We were friendly with the people who kept the pub, their name was Kemp, and when they told us they were leaving they suggested we put in for it, so we did. When I went down there Gus Jensen was in the *Rising Sun*, and me in the *Gas House Tavern*, and I believe

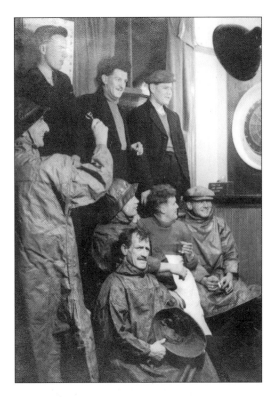

*Outside the Gas House Tavern in the early 1950s.
(Left to right) 'Darby' James, 'Young Darby' James,
unknown, Alice Brady, Fred Brady, unknown.*

*The Landlubbers versus Fishermen darts match, held in the Gas House Tavern just after the Second
World War. (Top left) Billy Ayres, Ted Boon, Sadie Springer. (With dart) 'Young Darby' James,
(sitting) Bob Prettyman, Georgie Prettyman, 'Lemon' James, (front) 'Dough' Clark.*

*The darts match must have been a busy night at the Gas House Tavern, as this photograph shows
another group there on that particular occasion.*

there was one further along, the *Dutch Hoy*, but that closed down, and then there was the *East of England*, which was a club by then and that's all the pubs there were down there by that time."

"The *Gas House Tavern* was my first pub. When we took it there were two little cottages on the side of the pub and my husband and a gang pulled them down and we made a little beer garden there. We lived upstairs but the kitchen was downstairs until after the flood. We were right opposite the old gasworks and we used to make a good living from them as their workers would pop over for a pint or two every day. I made tea and rolls twice a day for the Birds Eye people, and the shoe factory, and old Daisy Dinks was a regular."

"It was an interesting pub, and the people down there were the salt of the earth. Tough as nails they were. If it hadn't been for the flood I think I would have stopped there, but every time the wind got up I used to get frightened. I'll never forget that gale that blew that night. I stood there washing the glasses at the sink and I saw this water bubbling up and I thought, crikey, the blinking drain is overflowing. 'Course, when we looked out the bar door, the sea was coming up the road, you've never seen anything like it! And there was me, putting my foot over the drain to try and stop the water. We had seven foot of water in that pub, the firemen had to come and pump us out. Harry Burgess, he was the coxswain of the lifeboat, he came down in a little rowing boat. He said, 'Alice, I've come to take you up mine'. And I looked out the door and I said, 'Not on your Nelly! I can't swim', so my husband and I went upstairs till they got the water out. You ought to have seen the muck the flood left behind. It took us ages and ages to get rid of that, although we had a lot of help. We had a bogey stove in the middle of the bar, run by coke, and because the people

The Gas House Tavern on the day after the flood 1st February 1953. "We had seven foot of water in that pub," remembers Alice Coleman, formerly Mrs Brady, who was the landlady at the time. "I had the Gas House Tavern for about four years but after the flood I couldn't settle. Whenever it was windy I used to get nervous so when the Blue Anchor in the High Street came on the market I went for that."

The Gas House Tavern was situated in Wilde's Street. The earliest record of this establishment goes back to 1855 when Charles Goldmith, a beer retailer, lived there. After the Second World War it became one of the last two remaining pubs on the Beach before it was demolished in October 1967, shortly after the picture below was taken.

round our little area couldn't get any cooking and that done I had a big saucepan on there, and made saucepans of pea soup. I had the *Gas House Tavern* for about four years but after the flood I couldn't settle. Whenever it was windy I used to get nervous so when the *Blue Anchor* in the High Street came on the market I went for that. I think Billy Brown had it for a time after us."

John and Evelyn Baldry were licensees during the 1960s. "We used to live at 51 East Street," John recalls, "which was right near the Bethel. We were ten years in the cottage . . . We took over the *Gas House Tavern* in 1962. Russell and Queenie Kemp had it before Alice and then Billy and Emma Brown took it over for a while and we had it from 1962 to 1966. After us Keith Reed had it till it closed. We lived upstairs where there was a large lounge and three bedrooms and a bathroom. There was a back yard beer garden."

Evelyn remembers, "We had a good four years in there. It was during the time that the fishermen used to wear their coloured suits. It was a good family pub too. Fishermen and families. Tony Jensen, John Catchpole, who's now the coxswain of the lifeboat, Peter Gibbons who was another lifeboat coxswain, they all used the *Gas House*. The crew of the *Pioneer*, the ship that went down, they used to be regulars. We were there in the *Gas House* when that happened. It was terrible."

John continues, "Alfie Hall, Dick Hall, Jamie Lake, all used to come in. 'Umshi' Norman, he was a regular too. Then there were the 'ladies' of the Beach, Daisy Dinks and Maudy Linder, they were always in. Sonny Pickess, he used to help us to serve in the bar, Jean Keable used to wipe the glasses. Sometimes when the fisher boys didn't want to go to sea they wouldn't go into the bar for a drink in case the ship's husband came after them so they went in the room at the back. Christmas time when Birds Eye knocked off you couldn't move in there the bar was so full. A horse and dray visited the pub every summer, as publicity for Stewart and Patterson pubs."

Evelyn adds, "Sometimes I used to have to go out of the back door, and round to the side door in the pub, because I couldn't get through, we were so busy, people were all in the passageway."

The *Rising Sun* stood opposite the Herring Industry Cold Store on Whapload Road and was the last surviving pub on the Beach, closing on the 4th November 1968. "The *Rising Sun* was in my uncle's family for forty years," says Ron James, who after the Second World War opened the *Kumfy Kafe* in premises which had once been occupied by the *Flowing Bowl* pub. "My uncle was a Burwood, and in 1940 he took his life. He was so traumatised by the war starting; he'd been through the first one and he was so scared of doing it again, then the pub came out of the family and he took his own life."

"It was a lovely pub," Ron recalls. "Uncle Jimmy was awarded the cleanest pub in Lowestoft around 1937 and when I was a little boy I used to have the job of wheeling a barrow down the beach and filling it up with sand which was for throwing on his bar floor. Every morning he used to be up before six, sweep all the sand up, put fresh sand down, then he used to go outside and wash down and polish the wall which was red tiles up to the window-sills, and then he'd scrub the pavement. That was a lovely pub that was."

"I can remember they used to have what they called a 'Didlem' Club. That was about a penny or tuppence a week, and they used to have a 'do' at Christmas in the Smoke Room and of course no little children were allowed but being as it was my uncle, he used to let me go behind the bar, sit on a stool and listen to them. They used to have an accordion player and the old boys used to get drunk and dance on the table."

The Burwood name had a long association with the *Rising Sun*, one of the first landlords being James Burwood. By 1863 the pub had been taken over by Bob Hook and by 1883 it had passed to Robert Carver Butcher. In 1896 the pub returned to the Burwood family, with George Henry Burwood becoming landlord in 1902, succeeded by Ron James' uncle, James William Burwood in 1913.

In 1940 Burwood was succeeded by George Buck, who had run a shoe repair shop on the Beach for many years. His son, John, recalls, ". . . My Dad had the *Rising Sun* after Jimmy Burwood. Burwood died shortly after, I can remember he went to live in my aunt's old house, at the back of Vigilant Cottages. It was there where he killed himself, cut his throat. Before he took the pub on my Dad had run a shoe repair shop in Anguish Street since two or three years after the First World War. He had the *Rising Sun* for a couple of years at the start of the Second World War and then Alfred Tungate had it and then Gussie Jensen took it after him."

"The *Rising Sun* became too much for my Dad at the time. You see, although he was in his forties and had been in the First World War, he had to register for service. By trade he was a shipwright so he registered and had to go and work in Richard's shipyard. So he was running the pub and working at the shipyard. Then he had to do fire spotting at night-times and although my mother and aunt helped, it was all a bit too much for him, so he packed the pub in. But not for long; he had the *Greyhound* and then the *Triangle* after that."

By 1952 Gus Jensen had become landlord of the Rising Sun, but in 1955 the tenancy passed to George 'Bloater' Nicholson. Bloater's daughter, Mrs Edna Mortensen, recalls, "My father took over the pub in February 1955 and he came out in 1967. He was a trawler skipper before that. He'd been at sea since he was fourteen. I only lived down there a year, but I was down there every day after we moved. I had two brothers, Fred and John. There were four bedrooms over the pub, absolutely freezing cold, no central heating or anything. We weren't there during the 1953 flood but all round the pub, especially in the front room, whenever we had the slightest bit of damp you could see where the water had come up to on the walls. Salt would come out of the walls. Of course, it had been treated, the brewery did all sorts of treatments, but they couldn't stop this salt coming out. All round the cellar walls too. The building was never the same again."

"Dad used to let all the Scottish fishermen in on Sunday mornings at ten o'clock. You weren't supposed to but they all used the back gate, and the bar was quite full by half-past ten, they all liked the whisky! In October and November all the smoke houses round there used to smell of kipper smoke. I didn't mind that, I thought it was lovely. I used to like living down there. My Dad kept his hand in at fishing, sharing a boat with the landlord of the *Belvedere*. He still went herring fishing and longshoring in October with a friend of his and my husband looked after the pub at night-times and my mother would have it during the day."

"There was a fireplace in the bar which I think someone bought when they pulled the pub down. That fire was so stoked up in the winter that you couldn't get near it after a while. There were some carvings of dogs' heads on the wall too but one of the main features of the pub at this time was the 'model cabin' which had a magnificent layout of model boats which were made by Bill Carr, who was a local fish packer."

In The Rising Sun, (back row) 'Twee' Swan, Johnny Rose, Billy Thorpe, Jack Saunders, unknown, Billy Capps Jenner, Mr Tuck (Hon. R.N.L.I. Sec.) (second row) Hilda Burgess, Florrie Tuck, Mrs Saunders, Vernil Tuck, Harry Burgess, Tommy Knott, Bob Capps Jenner. One of the main features of this pub was the 'model cabin' which had shelves decorated with model boats which can be seen at the top of the picture. These models represented the boats which sailed out of Lowestoft since 1900, from the old drifters to the diesel trawlers. "You used to have to put a penny in the slot and the room went dark and all the ships lit up," recalls Edna Mortensen, "it was a real feature of that pub . . ."

"The models of the boats were there when my Dad took over the pub from the previous tenant who was Gus Jensen," explains Mrs Mortensen. "You used to have to put a penny in the slot and then the room went dark and all the ships lit up. It was a real feature of that pub. I think my Dad sold them when he left, to a pub in Orford." The models represented boats that had sailed out of Lowestoft since 1900, from the old drifters to the steam trawlers of the First World War and between the wars period, to the modern diesel trawlers. There was also a model of the *Girl Pat* which Skipper Osborn of Lowestoft made famous with his round-the-world exploits. There were models of boats lost at sea and models of both the Ministry of Agriculture and Fisheries research ship and the Naval Fishery Protection vessels.

"There was also a lovely clock on the wall," continues Mrs Mortensen, " a big old wall clock, and it was the sun coming up over the water, the rising sun, I don't know what happened to that. He used to have jars of whelks and cockles on the bar. The *Rising Sun* was on the site of what is now Karpet Kingdom."

Perhaps one of the biggest nights at the *Rising Sun* was on 4th February 1956, when the pub was visited by the BBC television programme, *Saturday Night Out*, said to have been the first live broadcast from Lowestoft. Three cameras were positioned on the premises, one covering the street, alley and bar through the window, another was behind the bar, covering the bar room, while a third was used to film some fishermen's wives in the lounge.

Mrs Mortensen has kept a copy of the working script used during the filming of that programme. She recalls, "I can remember Robert Beatty coming down and making his *Saturday Night Out* programme from the pub. The picture was taken of some wives sitting in our front room, talking to their husbands at sea, via the radio. They had a fishermen's waveband then that they could talk on. My father is on the left. It was broadcast live and the pub was packed out that night. My husband and I, we couldn't get in the bar it was so crowded, we had to go up and look in Morling's window, to see it on television."

The forty minute programme began with Robert Beatty, standing on a wet pavement in front of a plain brick wall on which was pasted an old and torn Fishermen's Week poster, announcing, "Welcome again to *Saturday Night Out*. Tonight we are with the fishermen of Lowestoft – a famous old fishing port in East Anglia where the sea has provided the main means of livelihood for hundreds of years." Then there were a few shots of wet cobble stones and a cat eating fishheads, two old fishermen coming down an alley together, then a shot of the trawler *Lowestoft Lady*, while Beatty gave a brief description of the town and its fishing. The programme then switched to the interior of the pub with Beatty inviting the viewers to, 'Come into the smoke room of the *Rising Sun* in the original old Lowestoft fishing village and meet some of these fisherfolk . . .'

Beatty then interviewed 'Bluey' Last, Mrs Last, Alonzo Mewse and Bill Carr, the modelmaker, at one table before moving over to Barney Smith, 'Tosher' Moore, and Billy Thorpe at another table, drinking and chatting while Bloater Nicholson served them drinks. Also featured on the show were the wives of the crew of the *Lowestoft Lady*, the skipper's wife, Mrs Reader, the mate's wife, Mrs Soloman, Mrs Randlesome, wife of a deckhand, and Mrs Cook, who had gathered in the lounge for a 'staged' conversation with their husbands on the trawler waveband and an interview with Robert Beatty. What then followed was a piece shot on the deck of the Lowestoft trawler, with Bob Danvers Walker on board, describing the conditions and work of a fisherman.

The forty minute programme ended with Beatty at the quayside with some fishermen's wives waiting for a sistership of the *Lowestoft Lady* to come into the

'Bloater' in the front room of The Rising Sun, with the fishermen's wives who were interviewed by Robert Beatty on 'Saturday Night Out'. Left to right: 'Bloater' Nicholson, Mrs E. Cook, Mrs Reader, Joan Soloman and Mrs Randlesome.

harbour. As the crew and relatives walked away down the quayside Beatty, the skipper of the boat and his wife went to an awaiting car and Beatty asked, "Is there anything you would like to say to our viewers before we go for a well earned drink at the *Rising Sun*, skipper?" To which the skipper's scripted reply was, "Yes. We're all very glad to have had you at Lowestoft and I hope that you people at home have enjoyed seeing something of what it takes to get good fresh fish to you. To any youngster who's interested – if you are prepared to work and know in your heart that you want to fish – come and join us and welcome."

Mrs Mortensen remembers, "We got a telegram later, from Peter Webber and Robert Beatty at the BBC, saying, 'Magnificent show, congratulations and thanks to our trawlermen, it was really great, the offshore sequences were fine'."

Bloater Nicholson ran the *Rising Sun* for nearly twelve years before he made the decision to retire. On 15th September 1966, Bloater spoke to the Eastern Evening News, at a time when the *Gas House Tavern* had only just closed, and he had witnessed the decline of the Beach Village. "There are no locals left now," said Bloater, "it's all passing trade – people working down here, lorry drivers and that sort." He admitted he would be glad when the area was cleaned up. "You get all sorts in empty houses, old ones and youngsters and no-one knows what they get up to."

The *Rising Sun* was taken over by Reg Reynolds and kept open for a further two years until 4th November 1968, when there was a memorable last night. Trevor Collis, who worked at the fish market during this time, well remembers this occasion, "The place was packed. They really drank the place dry that night. One chap had to go to work at six in the morning and only got an hour's sleep! Another chap was really drinking and there were so many people there that when he wanted to go to the toilet, they lifted him over their heads and he was passed along by the crowd. Every other record was the Animals' old song, *House of the Rising Sun*, or *Those were the Days* by Mary Hopkin. There was a Japanese flag outside. Those certainly were the days."

Looking down Whapload Road in the late 1960s.

The Dutch Hoy was situated on Whapload Road opposite the Eagle Brewery. This pub was established by 1853 and was then kept by Isaac Capps, although later this was run by the Yallop family. In 1931 these premises became Nellie Gibbs' grocery shop which remained here until the building was bombed during the war.

Next door to the Dutch Hoy was the Waggon and Horses, which was open by 1840 and still trading in 1906.

The Sailors Return was situated at 24 Anguish Street and was recorded as far back as 1855 when it was kept by Mrs Elizabeth Capps and William Burwood Capps. In 1927 this building was converted into a dairy by Joseph Flertey who moved there from his previous premises at 89 Whapload Road.

Public Houses

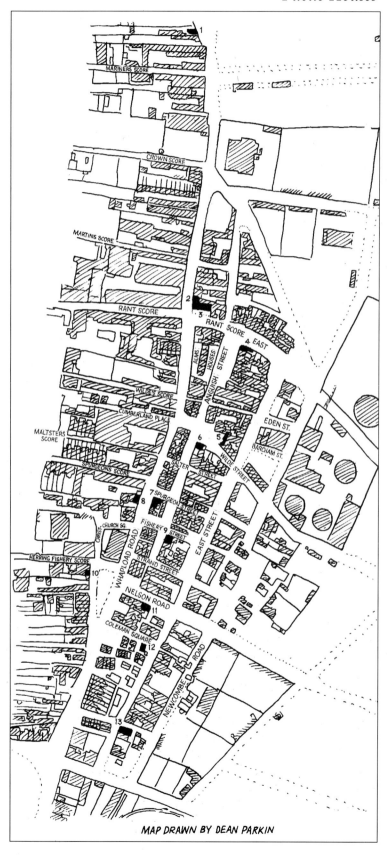

MAP DRAWN BY DEAN PARKIN

Here's a list of the thirteen public houses which were located in the Beach Village based on original research by Jack Rose and Ivan Bunn.

1. *East of England Tavern* stood in Whapload Road opposite the present-day Birds Eye cold-store. It was first recorded in 1879 – demolished in 1967.

2. The first record of the *Dutch Hoy* was in 1853. This pub stood opposite the old Eagle Brewery where the Birds Eye office now is.

3. *Waggon and Horses* was next door to the *Dutch Hoy*. First recorded in 1840 it was still trading in 1906.

4. *Flowing Bowl* was situated on the corner of Anguish Street, and can be found recorded in 1863. Remained as a pub until 1932 when it became a working men's social club. After the war the premises became the *Kumfy Kafe*.

5. *Gas House Tavern* stood in Wilde's Street, close to Cumberland Square. The earliest record of it dates from 1855 and it was one of the last two pubs left on the Beach Village when it closed in September 1966 and was later demolished.

6. *Sailors Return* was on the corner of Anguish Street and Wilde's Street and was there by 1855. In 1927 this was converted into Joseph Flertey's dairy.

7. *Rising Sun* stood opposite Herring Industry Cold Store on Whapload Road. This was the last surviving pub on the Beach Village and closed its doors for the last time on 4th November 1968.

8. *Fishermen's Arms* was situated opposite the *Rising Sun* and had been established by 1840, continuing until 1922. The premises were then used by Hammond's fish and chip shop until 1938 before finally being demolished after the Second World War.

9. *Suffolk Fishery Tavern* was in Anguish Street. This pub was de-licenced in 1927.

10. *Mayfly Inn* was next to the shop at the bottom of Herring Fishery Score. In 1865 a William Alexander lived here who described himself as 'beer retailer and hairdresser'.

11. *Princess Royal* was on the corner of Nelson Road and East Street. It was completely renovated in 1927 before closing in the early 1930s.

12. The exact location of the *Inkerman Arms* isn't known. It is thought to have been situated in the area where the Inkerman Cottages are believed to have stood, on a site which became part of Beeton's Net Works.

13. The *Balaclava* probably stood close to the *Inkerman Arms*, on the site of Reynolds & Hurrens Fish House.

Another public house, although not strictly speaking in the Beach Village, could be located nearby. The *Canteen* is thought to have been Bow House in Old Nelson Street, and was last recorded back in the 1820s. This was so called because it served the soldiers who manned the fort opposite during the 18th century.

12

Beach Life

"You wonder now how you lived there. I can remember
sitting round the table for dinner, and I had to sit
in one particular corner because I was the smallest one
and that corner was only big enough to hold me."

BERT PRETTYMAN

In 1954 Jean Mitchell had her first daughter at her mother's house, at 19 Wilde's Street, "Although we had no bathroom, and outside water and toilet, I had her at home. We had no sterilising units for bottles or fridges to keep food fresh yet food poisoning, or unhealthy babies, was hardly heard of. You sterilised the teats of the bottles in cups of boiling water."

You could be born on the Beach and die there too, as before the Second World War the Village had both a midwife and an undertaker. "We had a lovely midwife," recalls Lydia Cullen, "I don't know whether she had any medical certificates but she was very busy bringing a lot of babies into the village. She always wore a great big white apron. She was a very plump woman and very kind and meticulous in her work. Her name was Mrs Osborne." Indeed, Mrs Osborne's son, known as 'Bimbo', said his mother was very well known on the Beach, ". . . and was known as Granny Osborne. She went about with her white apron and was at the birth of many of the babies on the Beach."

"If we were ill," remembers Jessie Hitter, "Mother used to give us syrup of figs or liquorice powder, dose us up with that. You used to have to pay for a doctor in those days, a pound every time he came." These were known as club doctors who, in the 1930s, charged two pence a week which covered you in case of illness, and one pound for the doctor to call. However, the Beach Village had its own cure for anyone with breathing difficulties. "People who found it hard to breathe used to come down to the Beach a lot, sometimes from abroad," remembers Ronny Wilson. "They came to smell those gasworks and that was supposed to make them breathe a lot better. They thought it would help to clear the chest."

If anyone was ill, it wasn't long before the whole Village knew about it, and in a small community such as this, where everyone knew each other, births would be widely celebrated, while a death could cause the whole Village to grieve, such as the tragic case of Ronny Wilson's brother, Victor, who tragically drowned when he was eleven years old in December 1927. Ronny recalls, "My brother and the boy Lark got drowned skating on a pond at the bottom of Fir Lane in Oulton Broad. My father told him not to go skating but he got his skates and went."

Lydia Cullen recalls another similarly sad incident, "I remember two young lads

The Hammond family, pictured at the rear of their house in Jubilee Terrace.
Back row, Mrs Jane Hammond, Mr Harry Hammond, Charlie Miller, Jack Barber, Jane Hammond.
Middle row, Clifford Hammond, Alice Hammond, Mrs May Miller (née Hammond) with daughter May on lap, Mrs Anna Barber (née Hammond) with son Lennie on lap, Harry Hammond (Junior).
Front row, Lily Hammond, Lydia Hammond (now Cullen), Stella Hammond.

144

aged about seventeen and eighteen, their name was Cracknell, and they lived near Christ Church. One afternoon they were riding about on their motor bikes and they had an accident. One was coming out of the car park at Battery Green and the other was going in. They collided and both were killed, it was a very tragic thing and I think the whole village mourned for a time."

The Beach Village had its own undertakers, the Adams Bros., situated in Cumberland Place. "They were carpenters and undertakers," says Leonard Adams, whose grandfather and uncle ran this business. "On the 10″ rafters that held the floor of the loft he would write in chalk all the nine day wonders that happened, wrecks, floods, etc. for all to see. His brother Richard (Dick) was a bit of a lad in his young days but he married a Salvationist who changed him, and he finished up as a preacher at the Mission Hall in Chapel Street. As the people on the Beach were poor, most of the funerals were processed by the charity board (parish) so the funerals that came their way were only about one every fortnight, although when they retired in 1931 they still had oak planks that had been bought by people for future coffins."

"I was born in 1919, at 13 Spurgeon Score," he continues. "My grandfather, with his son and war-widowed daughter, lived next door at No. 11, my grandmother having died before I was born. My father was a carpenter, my mother was in service and I had an elder brother. My father died when I was four years old . . . We were not allowed in the workshop when they had a coffin to rush through, but we did see

Cumberland Place was situated between Maltsters Score and Wilde's Score. The house on the right was where Adams Bros., the carpenters and undertakers, ran their business.

enough through the window – how they cut and steamed the sides to bend them, boiled the pitch and rolled it inside as soil proofing, and filled the cushions with sawdust. We would be given the job of taking the plate to be written by Mr Rose in Police Station Road, and we would take a barrow with the stools to put the coffin on in the house if it was a long way from the yard. The hearse and horse were rented from Watling's in Clapham Road. We knew when they had been paid for a funeral. Grandad would look through his pockets to see if he had an odd ha'penny, the workshop would close, Uncle Dick would find a job at his Mission Hall, and Grandad would go to the *Gas House Tavern* or the lifeboat shod and come back the worse for wear."

Fishermen were lost at sea every year, it was a risk that they all faced, but the Beach community was strong and families stuck together. "My father's brother was going to be my mother's husband," says Lenny Norman, "but he was lost at sea, so my Dad took over and married her instead. That's how it was then."

"There were three cottages in Spurgeon Score which had seventy young children between the three houses!" Mrs Rose Sansom tells us. "All the men went to sea. The man in the middle house was lost at sea, and between the three houses they brought up these seventy children. This will tell you what Beach people were like. They were the salt of the earth. Generous hearted and kind. The front door could be left unlocked all night without fear."

Large families would be crammed into small houses and one such example of this is illustrated by the Rose family who lived in Barcham Square in East Street. In the late 1800s this was home to two adults and fourteen children as a result of premature deaths and re-marriage. James Rose and Harriet Cone had married on 20th December 1858 and had four children, John William, Michael James, Emma Elizabeth and Henry George, but Harriet died and on 4th October 1874, James Rose remarried. His new wife was Ellen Ann Sheppard, née Reynolds, herself a widow with four children by her first marriage. They had a further six children, Edward Francis, Celia Annie, Ellen Louisa, James Richard, Harry and Charles Samuel. The girls slept in one bedroom, full of straw, and the boys in another. On Friday night the old straw was burnt and replaced with a new load.

Mrs Jessie Hitter recalls, "We used to sleep tops and bottoms, with these big families. At the most there were three bedrooms in the houses on the Beach, and we were lucky because we had three. When we lived opposite Christ Church, the house had an attic and my mother got two beds up in that attic and all the younger boys used to sleep in one and all the girls in the other. My two brothers that went to sea were in one bedroom and my mother and father in the other one."

Benny Wilson lived near Ness Point Works, the premises of Rist's Wire and Cables, on Whapload Road. He recalls, "In our family there were four girls and five boys. The house had four rooms, two up, two down." His brother George continues, "Four girls and five boys, we were sleeping head to toe, but that didn't mean a thing in those days."

"Our house was, for a family of four, small to say the least," says John Day, who was born in 1943 and brought up at 2 Canary Cottages, Whapload Road. "Even as a pre-teenager, I could lay on my back and my head would touch one wall while my toes reached the other wall and I could spring on the bed springs and touch the ceiling."

Yvonne Scriggins says, "My parents were married in 1926 . . . they had eight children and as the Second World War approached money, jobs and houses were

The Woodrow family who lived in Spurgeon Score and had twenty-three children.

The sisters Rose Sansom and Myrtle Porter lived in the house at the far end of this row in Newcombe Road. On the left can be seen Albert Spurgeon's shod, whilst at the end of the street is the shod belonging to Harris Allerton.

scarce. With eight children to feed and clothe it was a struggle to say the least. Home for them was a two bedroom house on Whapload Road."

Jean Mitchell came from a family with many Beach Village connections and was one of the last to leave the area in the 1960s. "I was born in 1933 and was nearly six when my father died at the age of 29 years and my mother and I, with my older sister and younger brother, moved to the Beach. My mother was Jenny Prettyman and we lived with her family at 55 East Street, next to the Little Bethel. She had married my Dad, Henry Keable, in December 1928. All my uncles were fishermen, my mother's brothers, Bob, Charlie and Jack Prettyman, all lived at 55 East Street till they married. Her sister May married Sadie Springer and her sister Edie married 'Oxo' Coleman . . . First we lived at East Street, next to the *Flowing Bowl*. Then, just after war broke out, we moved to 19 Wilde's Street. The house had three bedrooms, two downstairs rooms and a large 'wash house' with a coal-fired copper and one cold tap with a bucket under it, no sink. We had an outside loo. Our house in Wilde's Street was very damp, with lots of mice, and flying ants in the hot months."

Eric Horne spent his 1930s childhood at 4 Rant Score. "There were six houses in the terrace, with another two or three joined at a right angle. The cottages are no longer there, only the site remains. We had two small bedrooms, one living room known as the front room, and a very small kitchen. The kitchen had a cooking range (also used for heating), a brick copper with a fire underneath, and a double gas ring for hot water or cooking. Outside in the yard was the only tap, and the ancient lavatory. An old sink of sorts sat on bricks, but was unplumbed and never used. Opposite the back door was the coal shed and my mother's giant mangle."

"I was born at 8 Rant Score East, next door to the Jensens," recalls Joy Pearce. "Ours was a bit of a weird old house. It had a yellow stone sink just inside the kitchen door, and there was a cooking range in the kitchen. It had a little open fire in the living room. There were three rooms, and the front door opened onto the pavement."

Sheila Maye tells of the house where her father, William Almond, used to live. "William was born on 11th May 1908 . . . in 1912 the family moved to 3 Coleman Square. The house was tiny, two small rooms up and two down, with an outside lavatory. There was the luxury of gas light in the downstairs front room, but the rest of the stone-floored house was lit by candles and paraffin lamps. The small kitchen had an open coal fire, with an oven set in the wall beside it. All the family cooking was done there, including the twice-weekly bread making."

Billy Keith was born at 2 Cook's Buildings, "It was near to Sayer & Holloway's fish house on Whapload Road," Billy explains. "The house had two down and four upstairs, but the bathroom where we had to wash was outside. In the winter we'd get the bath inside the house. We had a tap outside and a tap inside, but all the washing was done outside . . . I had four brothers and two sisters. My mother worked in a fish house and my father was Scottish. He came from Peterhead and was the foreman in a smoker, Sayer & Holloway, and from there he went to Mummery's and then Arthur Easto. When I was about seven I had a mastoid, and Lowestoft's new ambulance came to get me. But they couldn't get me down the staircase, it was too narrow, so they had to take me out of the window."

Harriette 'Elly' Ellis (née MacKinnon) lived next door to the Keiths. She recalls, "I lived in Cook's Buildings. The Pitchers lived in one house, the Keiths the next one, and we were next door, and then there was the Francis family. Next to them were the Boardleys. I had two sisters and one brother. My father's family came from

The building in the centre of the photograph was at one time the Flowing Bowl public house which was situated in East Street, next door to where Jean Mitchell (née Keable) lived.

Eric Horne lived at 4 Rant Score, which can be seen to the left of the photograph (middle of the row with the partly painted frontage). "My mother had to pay 4/6d rent for our terraced four roomed cottage," recalls Eric. "Our house comprised two small bedrooms, one living room known as the front room, and a very small kitchen."

Rant Score East. In the 1930s the Turrells lived in No. 8, which is the house at the far end on the right of the photograph, next door to the Jensens.

Joy Pearce with her grandfather, Arthur Turrell, in the backyard of their house which was situated in Rant Score East.

Fraserburgh in Scotland. He died when he was 37, and then my Mum married again. My grandfather lived in Cook's Buildings, and my grandmother's maiden name was Cook, the buildings belonging to her family. I used to take the rent down to them."

Benny Knights, born in 1909, lived in Nobb's Buildings, a row of twelve cottages along Whapload Road, near the Gourock ropeworks. Benny recalls, "We didn't pay any rent for sixteen or seventeen years because we lived in a condemned house. We had no back door, no sink. If you wanted to go to the toilet you had to go twenty yards across the road."

Nobb's Buildings was a row of twelve cottages between 295 and 297 Whapload Road, reached by an alleyway which continued up the cliff and through a garden before coming out near 17 High Street. The Buildings were subject to a clearance order on 9th October 1936, and the last two cottages to be inhabited were Nos. 6 and 11.

"We never used to bother to lock the door," remembers Leonard Boyce. "A lot of those little cottages were only tiny places, more like dolls' houses some of them. Broken down places, very, very poor. Sometimes they never even bothered to shut the door, you could see right through."

As a child in the 1920s, Charles Oldman lived in Scarle's Buildings, which was at the back of Mariners Score and ran parallel to it. These were a row of fifteen cottages which were condemned by the council in 1935. "You wonder how you survived in a place like that," Charles says, "My mother's brother lived next door and at the back of each house where the stairs went up was a little window where they could talk to each other. There was a hole down between them, but you couldn't get out, it was all dark because of this building at the back, which was a fish house, and the wind used to blow rubbish down there, and you had to lower someone down to get it."

Dennis Leach also lived in Scarle's Buildings. "My family moved down there when I was four. We lived right on the corner, near the net store. Scarle's Buildings was a row of cottages from Whapload Road to an opening half way along Crown Score. There were a lot of cottages joined together, but for some reason ours was on its own. The one nearest to us, what we called our neighbours, housed the Songhursts, Dick Songhurst and his family. You went straight out of our living room into the opening. There was a little kitchen behind and you went up some narrow little stairs to the two bedrooms. Our windows looked out into the net store. Now and again, if we were short of coal, we used to go and pinch the coal from the net store."

Other residents in Scarle's Buildings were the Ellis family. Charles remembers, "Scarle's Buildings was dead opposite the Steam Laundry. You only had one door into the house, which was at the back, and Gouldby's fish yard was at the back of the row. You went to the door and down the yard, 30 or 40 yards, and there was a brick shed with a copper in it and that was where the washing was done. Let's face it, Scarle's Buildings were slums, there was no doubt about it. They were damp, you had a tap down the yard, lavatory down the yard, no electricity . . . I can remember old Harry Green lived next door, he lived alone but I tell you why I remember him, he had an alarm clock on a piece of rope instead of a watch. He used to carry this blasted thing about. For a time 'Puggy' Utting lived in Scarle's Buildings. He was a tramp really . . . a rag and bone man. He lived in a house but it wasn't much of a house. In this day and age it wouldn't be tolerated."

John Buck recalls, ". . . We were all like a clan down there, we lived in groups, my aunts were in a large circle more or less. We lived in Vigilant Cottages which were just off the south end of Whapload Road. Just in our row of cottages we were all related. My uncle, Frank Bunn, lived at No. 1, I lived in the middle with my Mum, Dad and one brother and two sisters, and my grandfather John Rose and my granny lived in No. 3. My grandad was Jack Rose's grandfather's brother so, you see, my mother was a Rose. I think my granny had seven girls and one boy. Later on they moved from Vigilant Cottages to the Alms Houses.

After my father came out of the *Rising Sun* we went and lived in Jubilee Terrace, we lived there for a little while. Boardleys lived in the one near the church, we moved into the middle one and the Gowers lived on the other end, next to Hammond's fish shop. We lived in four places on the Beach, Vigilant Cottages, the *Rising Sun*, Jubilee Terrace and in the row of cottages just past Gibbs' later shop."

The Tucks lived at 27 Wilde's Street. Beryl Clover remembers, "You can't believe now that we could ever have lived there. Eight terraced houses were there, how they all fitted in I'll never know . . . This house had four rooms, the tap was in the yard, the toilet was outside, and we had a wash house where we had to do our washing. There was no water or electric indoors, we had gaslight."

"Of course, in those days there were no mod. cons.," says Ruby Timberley, "and mothers would spend all day on Mondays at the wash tub having lit the copper fire, which was in a brick shed, to heat the water. The washing was all done by hand with hard Sunlight soap and soda. The ironing was done with a flat iron, which was heated on the fire in the kitchen range. In those hard-up days there wasn't so much ironing because nobody had many changes of clothes. But there was a certain contentment. No-one had anything to steal, so doors could be left unlocked all day, stealing was unheard of in our area."

Jessie Hitter remembers, "Saturday night you used to have to wash the clothes ready for Monday morning, because we never had extra clothes. You'd have a

Jubilee Terrace was a row of three houses situated close to Christ Church. The Boardleys lived in the first of this row, Matthew Boardley being one of four children. He recalls, "This house had two numbers. We lived at 1 Jubilee Terrace or 69 Whapload Road!" Jubilee Terrace remained standing until the early 1990s when the houses were demolished and the site became part of the Lowestoft Cold Store.

Vigilant Cottages were situated at the south end of Whapload Road near Canary Cottages. In the 1930s John Buck's family lived in this row, his uncle Frank Bunn was in the house on the left, John Buck and his parents in the centre, and John's grandparents, John and Harriet Rose next door.

There were many Roses in the Beach Village. John Buck's grandparents were Harriet Ann Jemima and John Rose pictured here at the rear of the Alms Houses. John was a Beachman and lifeboatman and was Jack Rose's grandfather's brother.

The Fishermen's Hospital was built in 1838 for £600. This was a row of cottages on Whapload Road, built for aged and infirm fishermen. Two additional cottages were built in 1907 and the buildings became known as the Alms Houses. In 1964 several stone plaques which were on them were removed and placed on the new Alms Houses which were erected near St. Margaret's Church, and these cottages were demolished on 14th February 1968.

Cumberland Square was near to the Gas House Tavern off Wilde's Street. The picture above shows the entrance to the square with Sadie Villa on the right. This was one of the two houses, the other known as Darby Villa, which were named after the residents, Sadie Springer and 'Darby' James.
Cumberland Square (below) contained some good examples of the cobbled houses which were built using stones from the beach. These five cottages were pulled down in October 1967.

Sunday frock, you used to put that away with your Sunday shoes. Put them away till the next week, you weren't allowed to wear them during the week. We used to have a big old copper outside in the wash house, used to burn the old boots and shoes. Then there was the old mangle you used to have to turn for your mother and the scrubbing boards which were used to scrub the fishermen's clothes when they came in from sea. It was hard work. I used to take linen down to the Denes if it was a fine day and put a linen line between the net posts. You weren't afraid anyone would steal your sheets and they were down there all day, no-one ever went and stole your things."

"After the Scots girls had finished each year, we used the pickling plots as our drying ground," says Bert Prettyman. "If it was a nice day and for some reason your mother hadn't collected her linen when it was dry, it would be taken in and folded and brought to your house so the next person could put hers up. Sometimes it would be ironed too, that's the sort of people we were."

Mondays were wash days at John Day's home. "It took all day to do the washing, drying, ironing and hanging up. We had a scullery with a coal fire under a massive metal cauldron which my mother filled with buckets from a tap in the back yard and I played being lost in the fog when the steam began spreading up from the bubbling waters. We had one of those heavy cast iron mangles and heaven only knows how my fragile mother managed to wring out sheets and blankets on her own."

"Then there were bath nights," recalls Michael Duncan. "The long galvanised bath hung on the outside wall in the backyard, and had to be brought into the dining room, put in front of a blazing coal fire and filled with hot water. When my younger brother came along, it was quite a long job getting bath night out of the way. The coal-fired boiler in the kitchen used to work overtime supplying hot water for baths and washing clothes. I remember helping my mother on wash days by turning the handle on the mangle. If I remember rightly, she did most of the fisher girls' laundry and their bed linen."

Jessie Hitter remembers having a tin bath in front of the fire. "I used to bath all my kids on Saturday. You used to have to fill your kettle and saucepans up with water, and after I bathed them I used to fill it up with some warm water and kneel down and wash all the kids' school clothes ready for Monday morning. Nine o'clock I used to finish after that lot. I used to get the kids to bed after I bathed the four of them."

Norma Wilson was one of three sisters in their Wilde's Street home, "When one of us washed our hair, the others would run out and get the water. We used to clean our teeth outside because the drain was right in the middle of the backyard. Our Dad used to walk down to the lifeboat shed or one of the pubs while we had our wash, that was his excuse!"

Houses on the Beach began to have electricity for the first time in the 1930s, but previously there were paraffin table lamps or wall lamps and before that candles. Mrs Fisher (née Thurston) was born on 22nd July 1904 and she recalls, "I lived in a house on Whapload Road, at the bottom of Crown Score. It was a one up, one down, and had a little staircase with a candle at the top."

Miss George lived in Snowling's Buildings. "This was the row of houses near Christ Church which they pulled down when they built the Central School. They were little houses, one room downstairs, one room up. There were benches inside to sit on, and a water tap outside."

Joy Pearce grew up in the 1930s. She recalls, "We had the gaslight, and the mantles were ever so fragile. You had two chains, either side of the lamp, to regulate the light." John Day meanwhile seemed unabashed by this new technology. "I loved lighting the gas mantles which would pop at times," John says, "and when our outside toilet got a flushing system, I played pulling the chain for hours."

Even when electricity was connected, it was usually only partially, and the older residents were unsure and uncomfortable with it. Colin Dixon's grandmother lived at 4 Wilde's Street before she moved to Hopelyn Cottage, next to the Alms Houses, in the late 1950s. Colin, who was born in the front room of the Wilde's Street house in 1941, remembers, "My grandmother's name was Katie Hull, her sister was Jessie Hitter and her brother was Tom Harper. Grandfather decided to have electricity put on in the Wilde's Street house which cost him £7. 10s. But that was only one main room and an ancilliary room, the whole house wasn't electrified. There wasn't anything in the scullery, which was the kitchen, and we still went to bed with candles although we had electricity. One of the funniest things about Grandma was when she went to bed, she would pull the cord to turn out the light in the main room, what we'd call the lounge now, and she'd pull the cord but still blow at the same time as if to extinguish the last bit of gas that was coming out."

Nos. 4 and 6 Wilde's Street. Katie Hull, Colin Dixon's grandmother, lived at 4 Wilde's Street until she moved to Hopelyn Cottage, and Miss Adams lived at No. 6.

"Most families used oil lamps and candles," recalls Mrs Timberley, "but some had gas lamps although they couldn't afford to use them as they had to buy gas mantles . . . The streets were lit by gas in the 1920s. We had a gas light very close to us on the corner of Strand Street and Anguish Street. The lamp lighter used a long pole and went to each street light in time for lighting up time, returning in the morning to put the lights out. He seemed a solitary figure, seldom speaking to anyone."

In the 1930s, gas cookers could be hired from the gas board for a shilling a week and were a lot cheaper to run than electricity. Coal fires were used in all houses as anything could be got rid of by putting it on the fire. "I can remember the men with coal sacks," says Jean Mitchell "on their head and shoulders, unloading the coal. We used to take a barrow and pick up all the bits they dropped. And every Friday we used to go and get a barrow of coke for about a shilling from the gasworks, which smelt terrible."

Money was still tight after the war, and in the early 1950s when Doris James was running the *Kumfy Kafe*, she had her own method of getting coal, "One of the drivers at the gasworks used to come in the cafe and sometimes he'd say, 'I'm on duty this morning, just watch out,' and he used to swing round the corner and lumps of coal flew off and I used to run and pick them up!"

Poverty and hardship had always been a part of Beach Village life. In the 1930s there was no family allowance, social security or old people's homes. "My father was a fisherman," recalls Mrs Hitter. "He died young and left my mother with ten children. There was no relief then, and old man Jarrold came round and saw my mother and he say, 'You've got a tidy room here, if you're hard up, get rid of some of that', and he say, 'If you can't manage, put some of your boys in the home'. My mother say to him, 'While I've got a pair of hands to work, I'll work for my children', and she did . . . If they were hard up they used to pawn the old man's suit to pay the rent with . . . used to go down old Lark's, the pawn shop. They used to all run to the pawn shop to pay the rent with, if not they'd be turned out. But we weren't unhappy because everyone was poor the same. We weren't envious . . . no-one was jealous of one another then because none of us had anything."

Most of the people on the Beach used the pawn shop at some time, as Ronny Wilson remembers, "They'd pawn the old man's suit. Then we used to get paid a ha'penny to run down to the market, have a look out to sea and see what boats were coming in. If you recognised one of the boats, you'd run and tell the woman, and she would nip in and get the old man's suit out of the pawn shop before he got in. There were no rows in the house that way."

"No-one had much money," Mrs Timberley agrees. "No state aid then. Mrs Burwood would sell one penny worth of rice or pickles or other bits and pieces. Some women took in washing from better-off families to earn a few shillings. There was a Mr Buck, a cobbler, he was kept busy repairing the boots and shoes of neighbours. Our Dad mended all our boots, he had a last. For a shilling, we could buy a piece of good leather from a shop in the High Street, perhaps enough for two pairs of boots. Dad also cut our hair and Mum's. We all had a basin put on our head to get the shape and boys and girls ended up with a fringe."

Being the main produce of the area, fish was the staple food in all the homes on the Beach. "My grandfather would say, 'Go down the market and ask for my fish'," says Leonard Boyce, who was brought up at the *East of England* public house. "Prime fish it was, anything, whatever he wanted. Of course, Ayers, being part-owner, said he could have it but they used to throw it at you nearly."

Charles Ellis recalls, "In those days they used to bring home as much fish as they could carry and even if you hadn't got a lot in the house, it wouldn't be long before someone was round with a cracked plate, with three or four cod or skate, saying, 'Mum says we've got too much fish, would you like any of this?' and you'd got a couple of dinners there for everybody in the house, beautiful fresh fish. That sort of thing happened. I remember my father worked at Maconochie's who used to make sweets, and he used to bring jars of broken sweets home. All the kids used to come down to my house before they went to school and they'd all get a handful of sweets."

Michael Duncan grew up in Wilde's Street, next door but one to the *Gas House Tavern*, until the 1953 flood. "I remember luxuries were very few and far between, but one thing we did have for tea was chocolate spread. It was my responsibility with my sister to set the table and clear away and wash up afterwards. Once when I went to the pantry to get the chocolate spread out, whoever had put it away after use had left the top off. A mouse had got onto the shelf and into the tub and all I could see were its hind legs and tail. The mouse was stuck and dead."

"A friend of mine was ill," recalls Hazel Boardley, "so my mother said, 'Take her this egg custard,' and when I ran in with it her mother said, 'Quick, I've just sent my little boy to get an egg and I shan't need it now,' and I had to run after this boy to stop him spending the money. It could only have been a penny-ha'penny but she couldn't afford to spend it."

"After the war my mother used to work in a fish house to help feed and clothe us," Jean Mitchell remembers. " We often used to buy two penn'th of seconds (kippers) for our tea, and at Slater's boneyard we used to buy six penn'th of chitlings." Jean was born and bred on the Beach, meeting her husband, Brian, at the Coastal Boys' Club which had been started in the Little Bethel by Charlie Curtiss in 1948. "We married in 1951," explains Jean, "when my husband went into the R.A.F. to do his two years National Service. We carried on living with my mother and brother at 19 Wilde's Street . . . Almost a year after our daughter was born, we were able to buy our first house at 8 Wilde's Street. My husband was out of the R.A.F. by then and as he had qualified as a bricklayer and plasterer before going into the R.A.F. he was working in the building trade with Leighton's in Belvedere Road. We bought the house for £175 from Tom Battrick who had a shoe shop in the High Street. He let us pay him at £1 a week. He didn't charge us interest but used to get Brian to do little repairs for him. It was a two bedroomed house,

Beyond the Gas House Tavern was 19–33 Wilde's Street. No. 19, where Jean Mitchell's mother lived, can be seen on the far left at the end of the row, while Vernil Tuck and his family lived at No. 27 which is the house with the white door in the centre of the row.

with a front room, middle room and a tiny kitchen with a sink and cold tap. The toilet was outside in a yard shared with two ladies, the Adams sisters . . . We moved from the Beach to Europa Road in about 1965 when a compulsory purchase was put on our cottage for which we received £350, so we made 100% profit on it. By now most of the people had been moved for the development of Birds Eye."

Since the end of the Beach Village in the 1960s, an almost mythical status has been given to the area and many, who have no knowledge of the Grit and its people, seem to imagine it as a cosy fishing village with picturesque cottages. It was the people who made this Village unique, and the indominatable spirit of the Beach Community is still very much alive and in evidence in the surviving 'Gritsters'. In 1992 the first of many Beach Reunions was held, arranged by Bert Prettyman. It was a well attended gathering of old friends, many of whom had not seen one another since the outbreak of the Second World War, but who still shared this bond with each other, a friendship which hadn't been broken by the intervening years. What brings these people together? Why was the Beach Village so special?

"There was more spirit than today," says Charles Ellis. "The Beach community had this spirit and when you think of the depression in the 1930s, that was a depression, and they needed that spirit all right."

"Doors were seldom shut or locked," Mr Day remembers, "We weren't afraid then of being done over like today."

"They say about the good old times, well, they were good times, but they weren't good in some ways," admits Lenny Norman. "Money was so scarce. I can remember people going to sea for weeks on end, and coming back with nothing. The Beach Village was a community of good people, everyone helped each other."

"Beach people loved one another," explains Harry Harper. "If someone was ill they cared, they'd help you, take your washing in and iron it for you. They were like that."

"You look back now," says Billy Keith, "and think, 'How did they survive with all the work they did?' but it was entirely different to what it is now. Everybody knew each other and it was a community, the friendship was greater than it is today. You try to compare it, but it was just so different."

The Dalley family at a Christ Church outing to Corton in 1931. Standing at the back, (left to right) Ruby, Lionel and May. On the left (seated) are Jack and Claude who is sitting on the lap of his mother, Lydia Constance. Ruby Timberley (née Dalley), who made a major contribution to this book, sadly died prior to its publication, shortly before her brother Jack.

Looking up Anguish Street circa 1900. The row of houses on the near right of the photograph was where the Dalleys lived, at No. 4, next door to the Suffolk Fishery Tavern which is pictured on the corner. Buck's shoe repair shop was situated in the small building where the crowd of people are standing. The premises which would become Moss's sweet shop are shown on the next corner.

Aerial view of part of the Beach Village in the late 1960s.

1 Chromeglaze
2 Birds Eye fish line
3 Birds Eye main factory
4 Birds Eye dinner line (formerly site of Eagle Brewery)
5 Squire's shop
6 Primitive Methodist Chapel
7 The Alms Houses

8 Hopelyn Cottage
9 Birds Eye office block
10 Gas House Tavern
11 Darby Villa
12 Sadie Villa
13 Cumberland Square
14 Formerly Flowing Bowl, later the Kumfy Kafe

Another view of the Beach Village around 1967.

1 Birds Eye cold store

2 Steam laundry

3 Birds Eye canteen

4 Birds Eye factory

5 Mariners Score School

6 Beachmen's lookout

7 East of England public house

The beginnings of the industrial estate which would engulf the remnants of the Beach Village can be seen in this aerial photograph taken in the late 1960s. The remaining streets of the Beach Village are in the distance on the left of the picture, whilst the net drying posts are shown to the right.

Chronology

1400s   During the reign of King Henry IV (1399–1413) the fairs and market at Lowestoft were held below the cliff.

1500–   There was a row of fish houses along the base of the cliff, connected by cliff paths
1600s   or 'scores' to the fish merchants' houses on the brow of the slope.

1540   A three-gun battery was formed on the beach near the Ness for the defence of the town.

1549   Kett's supporters siezed the three-gun battery and made off with them up Rant Score to make an unavailing attack on Yarmouth.

1600s   Since the reign of Queen Elizabeth (1558–1603) the sea had kept encroaching
near   the town.

1624   The first lowlight, lit by candles, stood at the bottom of Swan Score, now Mariners Score.

1644   10th March, Gillingwater states there was "a great and terrible fire which consumed dwelling houses, fish-houses, and goods".

1650   Large iron coppers stood out on the Denes, in which cod livers were boiled to extract the oil.

1676   A brick and stone lighthouse was built which was 40 feet high and 20 feet round.

1717   12th November, another sudden and terrible fire broke out, this time destroying Captain Josiah Mighels' fish houses.

1735   The first moveable timber lowlight was erected on the Beach.

1737   January, King George II landed on the north beach having been forced onto land by a storm at sea. He stayed the night in the town in John Jex's house in the High Street, having been driven by Jex up Rant Score.

1738   John Wilde died and bequeathed his estate to the town after the death of his niece, for the establishment of a school.

1750   Beach Companies in Lowestoft were mentioned in documentary sources around this time.

1779   The decayed moveable lighthouse was taken down and replaced by another structure. The lowlight by then had been moved to the Beach near Spurgeon Score.

1780s   Three Beach Companies emerged in Lowestoft, Denny's, Lincoln's and Reed's.

1788   Seven years after the death of John Wilde's niece, a schoolroom was finally built at the top of Wilde's Score.

1790   Alexander Payne was appointed master of the new free school in Wilde's Score. Forty boys were picked to join the school when it opened the next year . . . The Gowings established their rope walk, which ran parallel to Whapload Road.

1791–   Edmund Gillingwater records that 76 tenements were constructed below the cliff
1806   during this time. These were the beginnings of the Beach Village.

1801   February 27th, The first Lowestoft lifeboat arrived. However, the Beachmen preferred their own boats to this strange new boat and the following year she was moved to Gorleston.

1810   More houses were erected on the Beach.

1824   An RNLI station was established in the town . . . The building of the new Bath House was announced.

1831   The harbour opened . . . It seems likely that another school room was built at Wilde's School, with this date marked out on a wall with the bottoms of dark bottles.

1835   The Beach Companies were re-structured and the Old Company or Down Streeters, Young Company and North Roads Company were formed.

1837   The town's first gasworks were built near Ness Point by a Mr James Malam.

1838   The Fishermen's Hospital was built on Whapload Road.

1844   Samuel Morton Peto bought the harbour. He improved the harbour and joined the town to the railway, giving Lowestoft's fishing industry a huge boost.

1851   218 houses were inhabited in the Beach Village, with a total of 1117 people living there (583 male, 534 female)

1852   The gasworks were expanded.

1862   A collection commenced to raise funds for the erection of a church on the Beach.

1863   Names were suggested by the Paving Committee for the streets on the east side of Whapload Road.

1865   Trawl dock opened.

1866   Lowlight was moved to Ness Point.

1867   The old wooden lowlight was replaced by one of tubular steel, capable of being moved around the beach.

1869   Christ Church opened.

1881   White's Suffolk (1885) states, that at this time there were 441 houses and 2,755 inhabitants in the parish of Christ Church.

1882   28th October, tragic loss of life suffered on Black Saturday when the lifeboat crew refused to launch during a storm . . . A gas holder was built.

1883   Waveney Dock opened . . . A private lifeboat, the *Caroline Hamilton* was bought to prevent another disaster like Black Saturday happening again, although the vessel proved difficult to handle.

1886   Arthur Stebbings, in his guide book to Lowestoft, estimated that the population of the Beach numbered about 2,400.

1891   The Denes were purchased by the Town Council.

1892   Christ Church School built.

1893   18th November, the Lowestoft volunteer lifeboat, the *Caroline Hamilton*, was sold by auction despite the protests of the boat's coxswain, Edward Ellis.

1897   30th January, renewed flooding of the Denes . . . Sparrow's Nest purchased by the Corporation . . . Proposals were put forward for a railway to cross the Denes and also for a new pier which was to run out from the north beach opposite the high light. These plans were later scrapped . . . 28th November, The whole of the Beach Village was flooded and lifeboatmen who had put out to help vessels in distress returned to find their homes several feet deep in water.

1899   July, The Model Yacht Pond on the Denes was officially opened.

1900   The population of the Beach was estimated at 2,500 people, thirteen public houses and the full range of working buildings. The town's population around this time was 23,385.

1901   The proposal of a hotel on Whapload Road was put forward . . . The North Roads Company amalgamated with the Young Company.

1902   Work began on the first sea wall . . . To celebrate the coronation of King Edward VII the biggest ever bonfire was built in Lowestoft, erected on the north beach near the Bath House Road, later named Hamilton Road . . . July 10th, Beach Bethel corner stone laid . . . September 14th, opening service at Beach Bethel.

1903   Hamilton Dock opened.

1904   Another gas holder was erected.

1911   Some of the fourteen cottages in Christ Church Square were demolished around this time to make way for a new school.

1913   A record number of 535 million herrings landed at Lowestoft. The combined Scottish and East Anglian drifter fleet consisted of 1,650 boats.

1914   Whapload Road School, built at a cost of £6,800, was opened . . . A site next to Hamilton Road was picked for the War Signal Station.

1915   Coastguard Station built by the North Sea Wall.

1916   April 25th, During the bombardment of Lowestoft by the German fleet, one of the shells fell in Lighthouse Score but didn't explode . . . Abnormally high tides caused widespread flooding and wrecked sea defences.

1919   August, a welcome home feast for 3,500 soldiers and sailors wass held on the Denes in large marquees.

1920   January 20th, the council refused an application from Captain C. J. Clark R.F.C., for use of a portion of the Denes to land aeroplanes.

1921   7th July, Denes swimming pool was opened.

1922   The Old and Young Companies amalgamated for a year but failed to get on together.

1923   Lowlight dismantled after better buoyage of the channel renders the structure superfluous . . . A new sea wall was built at a cost of £250,000.

1925   Denes Oval laid out . . . 25th November, a record high tide of twenty four feet caused the whole Beach Village to be flooded to a depth of about two feet.

1933   The Council declared the Beach a clearance area saying that the houses were badly arranged, old, worn-out and dilapidated beyond repair.

1935   The Council announced that they were to redevelop the Beach area, with the idea of turning it into a housing estate.

1937   October, The Lowestoft Corporation's redevelopment scheme for the Beach Village began, with new houses being built in Lighthouse Score in front of the old cottages they were to replace. No more was heard of the scheme subsequently.

1938   February, The Beach area was flooded with huge waves pouring over the wall and onto the pickling plots and surging down Hamilton Road along its whole length.

1939   The Old Company launched their last yawl.

1940   The Young Company launched their last yawl.

1940–   The Beach area suffered bombing raids, with Central School and part of Wilde
1942   School two of the notable buildings to be hit.

1946   After the war, compensation for the loss of Beach Company property was used to establish the Lifeboat Social Club.

1949   A small depot was opened by Birds Eye in the Beach area for the preparation and packaging of fruit for their Great Yarmouth factory.

1952   The Birds Eye depot was developed into a complete production unit with further investment and growth following.

1953   31st January, water swept through four hundred homes in the Beach Village and other areas of the town in the worst flooding of the east coast in history.

1955   The local press contained details of the 'First Stage of Slum Clearance Programme' involving the whole area east of Whapload Road from March Cottage in the north to the Bath House on the corner of Hamilton Road.

1958   September, The Eagle Brewery demolished with Birds Eye developing the site.

1960   Birds Eye employed 1400 people at peak periods.

1962   Lowestoft ceased to make its own gas supply . . . Birds Eye employed in the region of 1500 at this time.

1964   The old 100-foot chimney at the gasworks was demolished.

1965   The most modern of Lowestoft's gas holders was built with a capacity of a million cubic feet . . . The present Lifeboat Social Club was opened in Hamilton Road to replace former premises in East Street.

1966   Many of the people living in the Beach Village had been rehoused in new housing estates in the town.

1967   Demolition of property on the Beach gathered pace. In October of this year, the *Gas House Tavern* and Cumberland Square were demolished among many other buildings.

1968   Demolition work continued . . . 4th November, the *Rising Sun*, the last pub on the Beach, closed.

1969   The last gas lamps in the town, three in Lighthouse Score, were extinguished for the last time . . . March, the former premises of Belfast Ropework Co. were demolished, with Birds Eye developing the site, as clearance of the area continued.

1971   New industrial buildings were erected on the area of the Beach Village. By this time few dwellings remained on the east side of Whapload Road . . . February, the houses on the corner of Whapload Road and Old Nelson Street were demolished . . . 27th April, The old coastguard station was demolished, with a temporary one replacing it.

1973   New coastguard station under construction.

1975   The old gas holders were pulled down.

1991   Controversy raged over the future use of the Denes following an application by Birds Eye Walls to extend their factory in Whapload Road. Permission was granted and building work went ahead.

1993   The Denes IV factory, built by Birds Eye, was opened.

✳   ✳   ✳   ✳

The Scores

There used to be twelve scores, but in recent years we have lost one and two halves. In 1979 the new Police Station was built over Frost's Alley Score, which was the oldest, and the lower half of Wilde's Score was taken by the Birds Eye Walls Factory, while Maltsters Score has been diverted into Spurgeon Score.

The Ravine
Listed as Gunton Score on a three hundred year old map and later known as Park Hill. It has also been referred to as Sandhill Score, Grene Score, Lopham Score, Girdle Score and Jesuin or Haliwater Score.

Cart Score
Known as Gallow's or Gibbet Score.

Lighthouse Score
Once called Lighthouse Hill. The last gas lamps in the town were extinguished in 1969 (there were still over one hundred in September 1968).

Mariners Score
Believed to have been named after Samuel Mariner who owned property there. Earlier it had been called Swan's Score due to the Swan Inn which stood there. This was the inn where Cromwell is said to have stayed when he visited the town to put down the 'malignants'.

Crown Score
Seems likely to have been named after one of the pubs in this area. At one time known as Lion Score.

Martin's Score
Named after a worthy of the town Thomas Martin, but was formerly Gowing's Score, presumably named after Gowing's Ropeworks.

Rant Score
Has also been called the Blue Anchor Score and Youngman's Score, due to Youngman's brewery which was located here in the late 1800s. The current name of the score has been connected to a Christopher Rant who owned property at the top or bottom of the score in the early seventeeth century.

Wilde's Score
Also known as Denny's Score and School Score. This score is named after John Wilde, who died in 1738 leaving all his money in estate to start a school, which was run until the start of the Second World War.

Maltsters Score
Named after the *Jolly Maltster's* public house. Once known as Salter's Score, after a local merchant, this led down into Salter Street in the Beach Village, where presumably the merchant had his premises.

Spurgeon Score
Named after a worthy of the town but was also previously known as both Titlowe's Score and Acton Score.

Herring Fishery Score
Seems to have been named after the pub at the top of it, but has also been called Christchurch Score, Porter's Score, Nelson Score and Spendloves Score.

Frost's Alley Score
Was also been known as Bowlers Score and Brown Score until just after the mid-1800s. It is now covered over, through the building of the new police station. This was the oldest score and said to have been the seaward end of prehistoric pathway.

MAP SECTION

*The following maps have been
researched and drawn by Ivan Bunn*

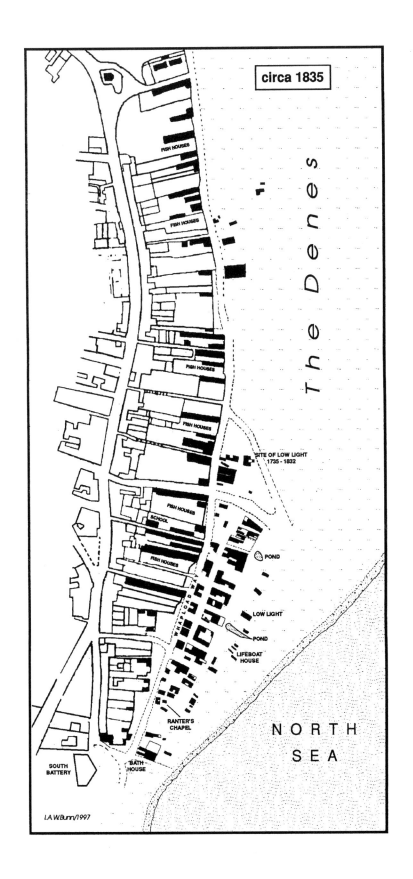

circa 1835

The Denes

FISH HOUSES

FISH HOUSES

FISH HOUSES

FISH HOUSES

SITE OF LOW LIGHT
1735 - 1832

FISH HOUSES

SCHOOL

POND

FISH HOUSES

LOW LIGHT

POND

LIFEBOAT
HOUSE

RANTER'S
CHAPEL

NORTH
SEA

SOUTH
BATTERY

BATH
HOUSE

WHARF ROAD

I.A.W.Bunn/1997

171

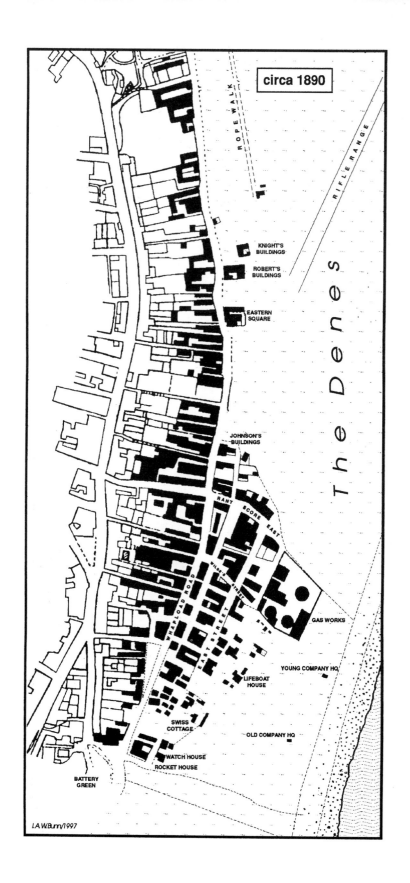

circa 1890

R O P E   W A L K

RIFLE RANGE

KNIGHT'S BUILDINGS

ROBERT'S BUILDINGS

EASTERN SQUARE

T h e   D e n e s

JOHNSON'S BUILDINGS

RANT SCORE EAST

WHAPLOAD ROAD

EAST STREET

GAS WORKS

YOUNG COMPANY HQ

LIFEBOAT HOUSE

SWISS COTTAGE

OLD COMPANY HQ

WATCH HOUSE

ROCKET HOUSE

BATTERY GREEN

LAW.Burn/1997

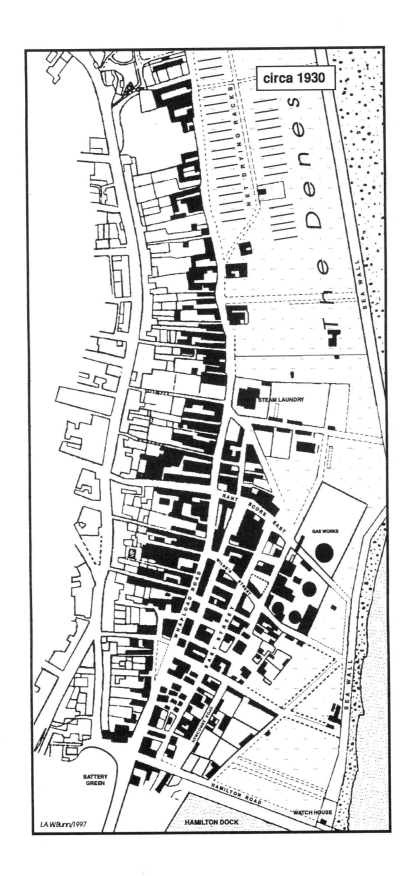

circa 1930

NET DRYING RACKS

The Denes

SEA WALL

STEAM LAUNDRY

RANT SCORE EAST

GAS WORKS

WILDE'S STREET

WHAPLOAD ROAD

EAST STREET

SEA WALL

NEWCOMB ROAD

BATTERY GREEN

HAMILTON ROAD

WATCH HOUSE

HAMILTON DOCK

I.A.W.Bunn/1997

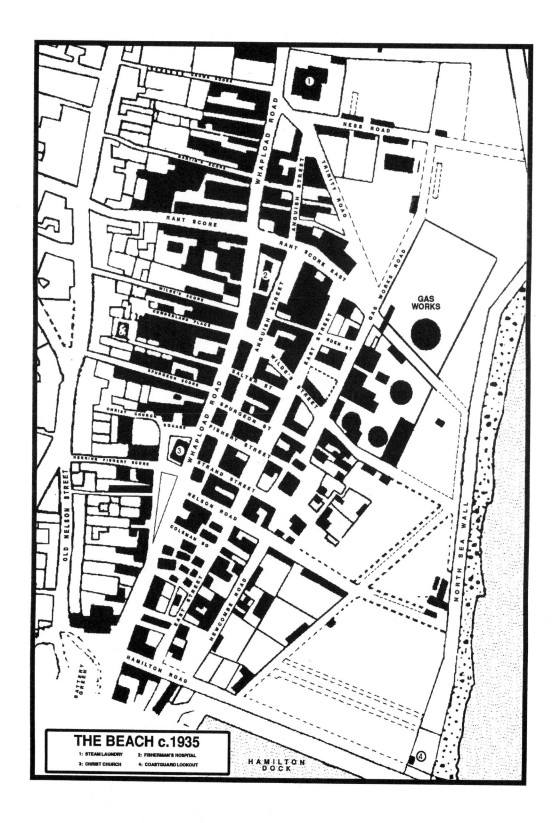

THE BEACH c.1935

1: STEAM LAUNDRY   2: FISHERMAN'S HOSPITAL
3: CHRIST CHURCH   4: COASTGUARD LOOKOUT

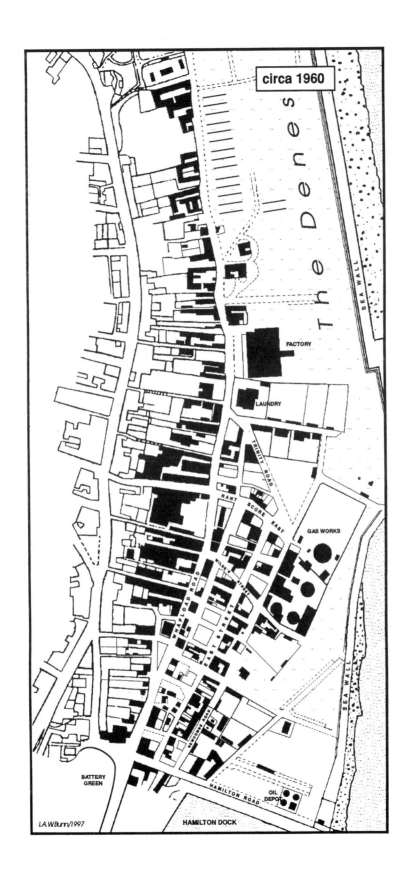

circa 1960

The Denes

SEA WALL

FACTORY

LAUNDRY

TRINITY ROAD

RANT SCORE EAST

GAS WORKS

WHAPLOAD ROAD

WILDE'S STREET

EAST STREET

SEA WALL

BATTERY GREEN

ANSCOMBE ROAD

HAMILTON ROAD

OIL DEPOT

HAMILTON DOCK

L.A.W.Bunn/1997

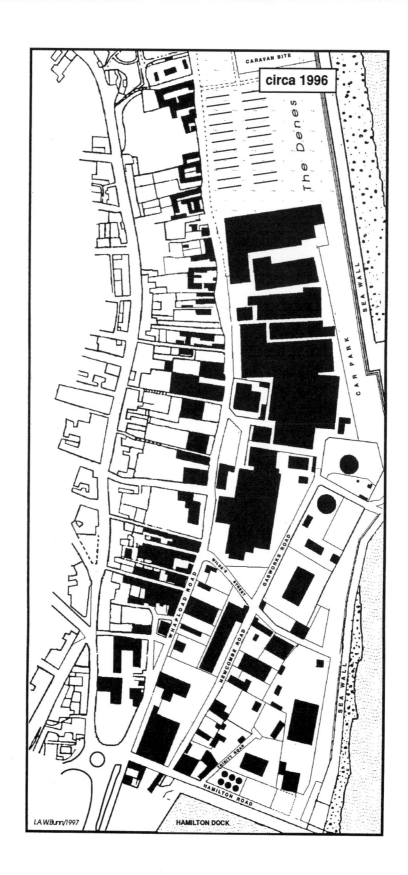

circa 1996

CARAVAN SITE

The Denes

SEA WALL

CAR PARK

WHARLOAD ROAD

WILDE'S STREET

GASWORKS ROAD

NEWCOMBE ROAD

SEA WALL

TRINITY ROAD

HAMILTON ROAD

LAWBunn/1997

HAMILTON DOCK

Bibliography

BARRATT, ANNE
The Beach – A Community Study

BLYTH, JAMES
Edward Fitzgerald & 'Posh' *(1908)*

BUTCHER, DAVID
The Cliffhanger *(EARD, 1983)*

BUTCHER, DAVID
Following the Fishing *(Tops'l Books)*

BUTCHER, DAVID
Living from the Sea *(Tops'l Books)*

COOPER, ERNEST READ
Storm Warriors of the Suffolk Coast, 1937

DUTT, WILLIAM
Norfolk & Suffolk Coast by William Dutt, 1909

DYSON, JOHN
Business in Great Waters *(Angus & Robertson, 1977)*

FLAXMAN, ROYAL
Wall of Water *(Rushmere Publishing, 1993)*

GANZ, CHARLES
A Fitzgerald Medley *(1933)*

GILLINGWATER, EDMUND
History of Lowestoft

GRIFFIN, STANLEY
A Forgotten Revival *(Day One Publications, 1992)*

HIGGINS, DAVID
The Beachmen *(Terence Dalton)*

HUSSEY, FRANK
Old Fitz *(The Boydell Press, 1974)*

JENKINS, FORD
Port War *(Panda Books Publishing, 1984)*

KIRBY, JOHN
Topographical & Historical Description of the County of Suffolk

LEES, HUGH
The Chronicles of a Suffolk Church *(1949)*

MALSTER, ROBERT
Lowestoft East Coast Port *(Terence Dalton, 1982)*

MALSTER, ROBERT
Saved from the Sea *(Terence Dalton, 1974)*

MARTIN, R. M.
With Friends Possessed – a life of Edward Fitzgerald *(Faber and Faber, 1985)*

ROSE, JACK
Changing Lowestoft *(Rushmere Publishing, 1994)*

ROSE, JACK
Lowestoft *(Panda Books Publishing, 1981)*

ROSE, JACK
Lowestoft Album *(Panda Books Publishing, 1983)*

ROSE, JACK
Lowestoft Life *(Panda Books, 1991)*

ROSE, JACK
Lowestoft Scrapbook *(Tyndale + Panda Publishing, 1988)*

ROSE, JACK
Tales & Tall Stories *(Rushmere Publishing, 1992)*

STEBBINGS, ARTHUR
Visitor's Guide Book to Lowestoft & Vicinity, 1886

TEMPLE, C. R.
Shipwreck *(Tyndale + Panda Publishing, 1986)*

WRIGHT, W. A. (ED)
Letters of Edward Fitzgerald to Fanny Kemble *(Richard Bentley, 1895)*

TOMKINS, HERBERT W.
Companion into Suffolk

The Lowestoft Guide by a Lady, 1812

The Illustrated Handbook to Lowestoft, 1853

Index

Figures in bold indicate pages with photographs.